P9-AFO-743

A Desert Harvest

A Desert Harvest

New

and

Selected

Essays

Bruce Berger

Introduction by Colum McCann

FARRAR, STRAUS AND GIROUX
New York

Farrar, Straus and Giroux
175 Varick Street, New York 10014

Copyright © 1990, 1994, 2004, 2019 by Bruce Berger
Introduction copyright © 2019 by Colum McCann
All rights reserved
Printed in the United States of America
First edition, 2019

The essays in this collection originally appeared, some in different
form, in the following publications: *Deserts: A Literary Companion*
("Heat"), *Amelia* ("The Mysterious Brotherhood"), *Orion Magazine*
("Comfort That Does Not Comprehend"), *In Short: A Collection of Brief
Creative Nonfiction* ("Fernando and Marisela"), *The Southwest
Review* ("Curse of the Adorers" and "Time Out"), *American Way*
("Black Pearl," "Salt on Their Tales," "Transition Zone," and
"Arrows of Time"), *Dark Horse* ("The Search for Mata Hari"), and *The
North American Review* ("Science, Environmentalism, and Music");
and in the collections *The Telling Distance: Conversations
with the American Desert*, *There Was a River*, and
Almost an Island: Travels in Baja California.

Library of Congress Cataloging-in-Publication Data
Names: Berger, Bruce, author.
Title: A desert harvest : new and selected essays / Bruce Berger ;
    introduction by Colum McCann.
Description: First edition. | New York : Farrar, Straus and Giroux, 2019.
Identifiers: LCCN 2018035767 | ISBN 9780374220570 (hardcover)
Classification: LCC PS3552.E7182 A6 2019 | DDC 814/.54—dc23
LC record available at https://lccn.loc.gov/2018035767

Designed by Richard Oriolo

Our books may be purchased in bulk for promotional, educational,
or business use. Please contact your local bookseller or the
Macmillan Corporate and Premium Sales Department at
1-800-221-7945, extension 5442, or by e-mail at
MacmillanSpecialMarkets@macmillan.com.

www.fsgbooks.com
www.twitter.com/fsgbooks • www.facebook.com/fsgbooks

1 3 5 7 9 10 8 6 4 2

CONTENTS

Introduction: The Piano Has Been Thinking, by Colum McCann   vii

HEAT   3

THE MYSTERIOUS BROTHERHOOD   5

COMFORT THAT DOES NOT COMPREHEND   11

FERNANDO AND MARISELA   29

CACTUS PETE   33

PHOENICIAN SHIPWRECKS   61

CURSE OF THE ADORERS   79

INFECTIOUS LAUGHTER   99

HOW TO LOOK AT A DESERT SUNSET   113

BLACK PEARL   115

THE SEARCH FOR MATA HARI   139

TIME OUT   169

THE METAPHYSICAL TENT   171

SALT ON THEIR TALES   173

WILDERNESS AND THE BURIED SELF   195

SIDEWINDERS ANONYMOUS   201

SLICKROCK AND THE BACH CHACONNE   205

TRANSITION ZONE   209

SCIENCE, ENVIRONMENTALISM, AND MUSIC   213

ARROWS OF TIME   221

INTRODUCTION:
THE PIANO HAS BEEN THINKING

Colum McCann

The American musician John Cage is credited with helping to pioneer the idea of the prepared piano, where unusual items—among them tuning forks, screws, spoons, rubber tubes, cardboard, plastic sheathing, bolts or paper clips—can be inserted on or between the strings to alter the nature of the piano's sound. The music, then, is changed. A note can be elongated or damped or even turned inside out.

The degree of change is dependent, of course, upon what is used to alter the piano, but these days just about anything can find its way into the belly of the electric upright or the baby grand. All one needs to shift the musical landscape is the hardware and a touch of imaginative genius. The first is easy enough to come by; the second is obviously a lot more elusive.

It should come as no surprise that apart from his work as

an essayist and a poet, Bruce Berger is also a pianist of the highest order. What I mean is that he actually plays the piano—at parties, at fund-raisers, in homes, in concert halls. He knows his music and he can command an audience. He might once have made a living as a musician, but thankfully he did not—instead, for quite a while now, Bruce Berger has been sliding a series of prepared pianos out into the literary landscape.

Berger appears to be a classicist at first—the sort of writer who might guide you into the drawing room and play quite competently, even beautifully, that which might be expected: the taut essay that opens up the possibilities that lie just beyond the windows. But spend a little more time listening and you begin to understand that he has indeed shifted the timbre of the piano and that the windows are, in fact, not only open but daringly so, floor to ceiling, north to south, east to west. He has prepared the language somehow, secretly, imaginatively, and it contains a sort of whisper to break the convention of the drawing room, to entice you outside to experience the wind and the light and the dust. The adventure starts here. How about wheeling the piano down the hill? How about swerving in and out of a line of neglected cactus? How about leaving it for a moment in that dormant arroyo? How about turning a corner in the town of La Paz into another street, into an alleyway just beneath the convent? How about sounding out a few notes of old Chicago jazz to surprise the living daylights out of your desert? How about turning the piano away from the sunset? How about throwing out a little discordant noise from the stars?

Which is to say that Bruce Berger is a literary surprise: he has prepared the piano and we might not ever know how he did it, but somehow he makes the local sound universal, and at the same time brings the universal back around to the local.

Bruce Berger has always been on the inside of the curve. As he says himself, he sank his first earthly roots not in the Chicago of his childhood, but when he set foot in the Sonoran Desert. After that, he floated in Glen Canyon before it was dammed; drove down the Baja Peninsula before it was paved; lived on Cannery Row before it became a boutique; and put down roots in Aspen before it appeared in the national gossip rags. He never clangs down too hard on these key moments in his life. He's not interested in drawing attention to himself; rather, it's what happens around him that truly matters, the otherness of life. There's no showing off or fanning out the coattails. He exists quietly in these places and times, and manages, then, to draw out their exact essence.

In fact, Berger owns a beautiful wood cabin right in the heart of Aspen, Colorado. What's fascinating about this is that there's little or nothing of contemporary Aspen to it at all: it's modest, it's shy, it's quiet, it's functional, it's humble, it hasn't come under the knife. It sits on a tiny flick of a path just off Main Street, surrounded by rental units yet somehow all on its own, with an incredible western view, a perfect reflection of so much of his work: right there, in the heart of things, yet isolated and thrown back too. (With a piano, of course, amid shelves and shelves full of neatly stacked books: I was lucky enough, once, to spend a couple of weeks there while writing a novel—I swear I can still hear the books whispering to the piano.)

"A taste for the desert is a taste for ultimates," Berger writes, "and death is the backdrop against which all we know comes to brilliance." There is often a whiff of sadness in Berger's work: the landscape under threat, the creativity stifled, the familiar house lost, the highway arriving or never even beginning, the mother figure passing away, the rare bird flitting from the branch.

At the same time he manages a sense of astonished being. Just because it's dark doesn't mean that the darkness prevails. Berger's world is not mannered or prescribed in any way. He discovers the gorgeous in the individual. He sees finality as a radiance. Upon coming upon a dying plant, he finds that "the more grotesque its deformities, the more humanly it seems to express itself."

All the essays gathered here—short and long—speak to Berger's glocal world, global and local both. He speaks to physics and environmentalism and a new form of mythology in the ordinary. The short essays read like pure poems. The longer ones allow themselves to dawdle awhile. There's a bravery in this. Picking a favorite is like picking a child, of course. I adore the mad genius of "Cactus Pete," for instance, and I am charmed by the pithy beauty of "How to Look at a Desert Sunset," but the essay that continues to rattle in me is "The Search for Mata Hari": read it and weep, and then exalt in layer upon layer of discovered music. Walk through the streets of La Paz in a new pair of shoes bought simply because one man can play the piano and many men and women want to listen. (I hope it's not too much of a spoiler, but I'd like to echo the last line, which reads: "That was extraordinary. I hope I can hear it again.")

Berger's writing is meticulous and beautiful, discerning and tender. It throws off the appearance of ease, but one can tell that an ocean of thought and craft has gone into each and every sentence. There is a lot of work underneath the words. His prose has sometimes been described as having a whiff of the intellectual, which in America seems to be a curse. It is indeed smart and clever, but he manages to avoid writing in rapt self-abstraction. It is as if Wallace Stevens has told him that the worst of all things is not to live in a physical world. Berger himself has often talked about writing toward the intersection of humanity and landscape.

His other concern is with language and its possibilities, its areas of recalcitrance and exhaustion, its capacity to aestheticize and therefore in some sense redeem quotidian reality. "Whether we're canyons or musicians," he writes, "we must dig into it and shape what we can." Indeed, the side canyons lead us to the deeper areas of experience. A large part of the charm comes in the buried humor—when it becomes apparent, it's like discovering ice in the middle of the hike, rare and refreshing. Sometimes Berger, especially in his self-effacing slant—honesty—can make you flat-out belly-laugh. You can almost see the little Chicago boy in shorts and mismatched shirt standing on the edge of the suburbs in Phoenix, ready to dash out and get marvelously lost.

Berger, now approaching eighty years of age, inhabits that territory that great artists finally carve out for themselves, using what he knows in order to go way beyond what he should possibly know. He takes the lived landscapes of his years and transforms them until they are something universal. He helps expand our degrees of consciousness and he gives a muscularity to what others have let disintegrate.

He has the touch of a poet, but for me his true talent is, and always will be, that he allows rather than instructs. He doesn't moralize. He steps us out from the known into the unknown, but we become our own guides on the journey. To paraphrase Tom Waits, or maybe, in fact, to "prepare" one of his more famous lines: *The piano has been thinking, it got me.*

A Desert Harvest

—UNLIKE COLD—IS ONE of those pleasures most keenly relished on the threshold of pain. It is oddly comforting to feel noon pouring down, to bake from beneath over bedrock, to find your marrow vaguely radiating. The best midsummer lunch is to gorge on enchiladas blazing with chiles, return to the car you have left in the sun with the windows rolled up, lock yourself in to steep in your own tears and sweat, then step out to find the heat wave has turned delicious. It is invigorating to walk over simmering gravel, feeling your soles come alive as they toughen, and baths are most relaxing when they resemble the first stages of missionary stew. Perhaps it is a desire to return to the womb, where we began for nine months at 98.6, that makes the warmth of alcohol so seductive, and one can comprehend—if not envy—the uncomforted who go through life sucking the eighty-proof tit.

Heat

To test my heat tolerance I once went into the desert when daytime temperatures were easing off around 107 degrees, to see what might transpire. I expected an escort of insects, lizards, snakes, scorpions and chuckawallas, all the cold-blooded predators warmed like me for action, but the cactus stood in stunned silence. The afternoon lay like a ruin through which I seemed the only moving thing. My eyes ran with salt, my thirst became pathological, and I fled homeward to chug two beers nonstop before I could explain myself. But did I dream of cool mountains, as I did in childhood? No. It is as an adult, exiled to cool mountains, that I dream of the desert.

IT WAS A CUSTOM in medieval times for saints and scholars to keep a human skull around to remind them of their mortality. That practice seems morbid as we plunge, youth-obsessed, into the twenty-first century, and the great bonescapes of Georgia O'Keeffe, their elegant folds of calcium and sky, remind us less of death than the deep cleanliness beneath the flesh. To see finality as a kind of radiance, one can turn to the desert not just for the melodramatic bones—which, despite cartoons, are few and far between—but for the quieter revelations of the vegetable world. Those unlikely green lives, each stranded in its claim to water, shed their skins to reveal still deeper miracles.

Cactus are among our most treasured species, yet only cholla has attained posthumous notoriety. The cuddly-looking shrubs—actually great fountains of barbed grenades, which, in certain varieties, nearly leap out for affection—strew in death

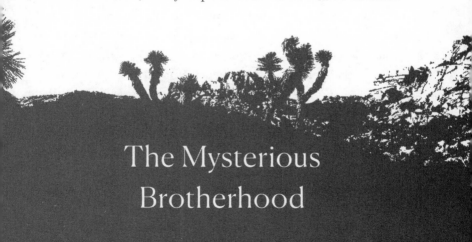

The Mysterious Brotherhood

the sections of their hollow stems, lattices of holes strung together by a woody fiber like asbestos. The delicacy of the recurrent patterns, the modulations of their holes, their rich patina make them sought after, and they grace the kinds of coffee tables where manhattans are served, find their way into flower arrangements, are positioned as a foil for foliage. They have been strung into lamps, hung up as hat racks, woven into macramé, tricked out as toy covered wagons. They have been stood on end and hollowed with ovals for the insertion of Heidi vignettes in isinglass, seashells and mother-of-pearl. They have in fact been conscripted for so many forms of kitsch, schlock and inventive bad taste that they seem some Sonoran revenge on deer antlers, abalone shells and Japanese fishing balls.

But it would be too bad to let their abuse obscure one of the desert's most moving cycles. Even as the cholla grows it drops its extremities, and if the pieces are not dispersed by wind, water, the flanks of animals or your pierced skin, they mass themselves under the plant like a field of charcoal. As the plant ages, the trunk turns black, the needles become brittle, and the skin begins to peel. The cholla may simply crumble, strewing bits of its stem among the decayed pieces, or tip intact into a small jungle gym. But if it remains on its feet, stripped to its fretted skeleton, it leaves a shape refined as sculpture, lord of its clearing, elegant by day and a spidery presence beneath the moon.

The prickly pear, less noble than the cholla, simply runs out of strength and lays its pads on the ground. If it is noticed at all, it seems a vaguely repellent gray heap. Trodden upon, it answers crisply to the shoe, a sensuous crunch like a bite of water chestnut or the slow dismemberment of a champagne cork. The serenity of its depths can call up visions of snakes napping in the cool, scorpions at rest, tarantulas digesting their friends.

Menacingly pale, it is most comfortably crossed after making a fair noise, in a state of high alertness. "Here we go round the prickly pear," said T. S. Eliot, and one can see why.

But reach down and examine a pad. The skin, turned sulfurous brown, peels off like cracked cardboard to reveal a mesh of fibrous sheets, each stamped with a similar pattern like a netting of veins and arteries, laminated sheet onto sheet. Each layer is a faint variation on the last as the holes rework their shapes throughout the pad. Fat green health hides the complexity of the prickly pear, and its disclosure is one of death's small rewards.

The smaller the cactus, the denser its spines, until one reaches the pincushion, one to three inches high, a white thimble usually nestled beneath some larger plant. The pincushion reverses the process by dying inside out, the flesh collapsing to leave a standing cup of barbed lace. Seldom recognized, the spent pincushion is a strange jewel, a crucible of woven stars each sprouting a hook like a talon, delicate as a doll's negligee.

Death on the desert: its forms are extravagant as the species themselves—the barrel's great mashed thumb, the organ pipe's burnt candelabra, the staghorn still more like antlers when stripped of its flesh. But for sheer pageantry the saguaro remains supreme. Largest of the cactus except for its Mexican cousin, the *cardón*, the saguaro reveals itself by painful degrees, breathtakingly. "What will become of . . . the huge and delicate saguaro?" asks Richard Shelton in his moving poem "Requiem for Sonora," but delicacy would not seem a prime characteristic of this stout colossus, one of whose arms, even as I watch in a suburban backyard, has been severed for months, is dangling by a thread and is blooming furiously. The saguaro can be killed, *is* being killed by destruction of habitat, but the individual, capable of storing up to ten tons of water, taking fifteen years to grow the first foot, surviving a half century before it blooms and attaining a height of sixty feet, seems resilient to an inspiring degree.

We know when an animal like ourselves dies: it is the moment when the heart stops beating. But when does a plant die? When it turns brown? When it falls? When the shape is finally obliterated? The saguaro begins to die even as it grows. King of its habitat, it is home to entire species of woodpeckers and flickers, which riddle it with holes for many other varieties of birds. The injured pulp secretes a thick shell, a petrified leather that offers a comfortable cave for the nesting bird while protecting the cactus, a hole that actually survives the plant in a collectible object called a desert boot. Branches routinely meet with calamity, suffer injury or fall off, to shrivel like crocodiles in the sun, yet the plant grows on, oblivious. The more grotesque its deformities, the more humanly it seems to express itself. By maturity the plant is pocked, gouged, may be missing or trailing branches or is gored to its bare ribs as if it were being eaten by darkness. Remorselessly it thrives. By the time it is actually ready to die, at the age of one hundred fifty or two hundred years, the saguaro may seem the butt of assaults past imagining.

At last letting go, the energy-collecting green skin turns sallow: the plant's least attractive phase. After preliminary jaundice the outer skin deepens, hardens, begins to crinkle and finally attains a kind of rich parchment. It extrudes a shiny black substance sticky to the eye, glassy as obsidian to the touch, as if it were being caramelized. Peeling skin reveals the inner pulp turning black, a burnt coral brittle to probing fingers. When tapped the skin now gives a report like a primitive drum, and could almost be played like a xylophone. Itself in sepia, the entire saguaro appears to be burning from inside.

At last the flesh is fallen, the skin strewn like old vellum, and the saguaro stands revealed: a white idea. If the specimen has many branches, or the ribs extend too far, the extremities will shear off, leaving stumps in a variety of crosses and elemental shapes. Occasionally a cactus boot, former home of some flicker or owl, will catch in the ribs, a hole become substance, revealed as if in a structural model. Though skin at the bottom may hold the freed ribs like poles in an umbrella stand, an immense rattle when shaken, at last the saguaro will fall. It is now only a confusion of hard skin, spines and crumpled flesh, with perhaps a stray boot, though even now the flung ribs may parody its shape in split bamboo.

Object of beauty, toy, curiosity, decoration, cheap firewood, musical instrument, home for scorpions, motive for metaphor—even a dead cactus has its uses. But a taste for the desert is a taste for ultimates, and death is the backdrop against which all we know comes to brilliance.

Cactus tells us nothing of what's ahead, any more than the death of a close friend: all they reveal is process, but process which retains, even in human terms, immeasurable beauty. Their odd green lives, if nothing else, bring to consciousness our complicity in a mystery that becomes, even as we reject it, our own:

> *Saguaros brave putrefaction like tough meat.*
> *Chollas strew black fruit while a skinful of char*
> *Peels into moonlight bleaching on its feet.*
> *The ocotillo collapses into a star.*
> *A mesh of fiber loosened by your nail*
> *Separates into bones of the prickly pear.*
> *Or lay your hands on a lung. Resemblances fail.*
> *Death is a common bond we never share.*

PEOPLE GROWING OLDER are said to return to the moods and culture of their origins, if not its actual place. I can't imagine returning to the moods of suburban Chicago, an origin I never even revisit. I feel that I sank my first earthly roots when I arrived at the Sonoran Desert outside Phoenix, at the age of eight. My family revisited it frequently during my childhood, and fate collaborated in my adult return. A number of years after my father died of the asthma that sent us to Arizona in the first place, my mother married a Chicagoan with a house outside Phoenix—to which they moved. I began visiting my mother and Frank over Christmas holidays. Then, when Frank acquired larger quarters—large enough for radically different people to live compatible lives—I started joining him and my mother for entire winters, lingering into spring. In my thirties I had managed to reproduce my season of discovery at the age

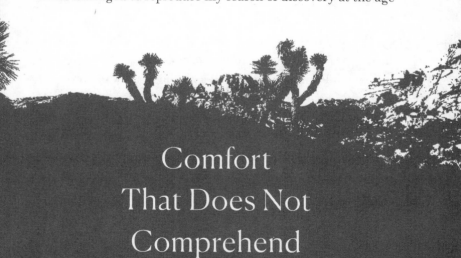

Comfort
That Does Not
Comprehend

of eight: I was living in the Sonoran Desert, five miles from where I first saw it.

The area was unusual for Phoenix, with the city's tradition of bulldozing the desert and replacing cactus with plants from back East, or California, or Australia, without questioning whether they look right, guzzle water or spread allergies. This particular neighborhood's pioneers zoned for five-acre parcels, with a premium on keeping the desert intact. In practice, they didn't let the cactus get too close to their living quarters, and in the case of Frank's purchase, the desert in front was fended off by a wall of oleanders surrounding a parking area, so that from my bedroom I looked out on gravel, then impenetrable leaves, then the gray slag of Mummy Mountain. In back, the requisite pool was blockaded by citrus, cassia, fig, laurel and loquat, punctuated by two date palms. The landscaper had effectively partitioned the property, with the desert on the outside and man in the middle. Such arrangements gave humanity a desert setting rather than a desert life, but most plant and bird species, rabbits and the inventive coyote withstood the holders of title insurance.

Because this new place was, in its minor way, a spread, it had live-in maintenance in the form of José, an aging Mexican whom Frank had employed since he first owned property in Arizona. A slow-moving man who stood with a hose to nonnative plants, José clipped when shagginess got flagrant and nursed his diabetes in a folding chair in the sun. I came and went, taking it upon myself, uninvited, to defend the property's desert, which needed only to be left alone. A guest of the interior, I found myself passing through the oleander curtain like a defector, rooting for what didn't need my help.

Winters that blurred without incident were rudely interrupted: Frank died after being assaulted by a stranger. Shortly thereafter, José entered the V.A. hospital with terminal diabetes: bonded for nearly a quarter of a century, he and Frank had almost departed together. The spread, bought by Frank alone, would ultimately go to his heirs but was my mother's to occupy while she survived. In the room vacated by José she installed a Vietnam veteran whose chief interests in life were studying electronics, reading the Bible and pulling weeds. One day, in a panic, I stopped him from tidying the exterior desert because he thought that native plants, being small, numerous and anonymous, were weeds. After three years of tending plants in return for a room, the veteran got his electronics degree and left. That was the end of live-ins. From this point on, the property was managed by a gardening crew that showed up one morning a week. My mother inhabited the spread alone until I appeared at Christmastime and realized that the cactus outside the oleanders needed a more active defense.

THE DESERT, OF COURSE, has a natural attrition rate that it was my privilege to watch. The oldest saguaro on the property, baroque in its profusion of arms, had an eye-level window where the pulp had rotted away from the ribs, showing how they hold the cactus up like rebar. Inflicting my cactus lecture on occasional visitors, I could demonstrate how saguaros branched, how woodpeckers gouged holes that cauterized into homey caves for other species—too frequently, now, invader starling—then lead the poor guest (mind the cholla!) to the demonstration cutaway model. "And this is how saguaros are built . . ." The inset was only a few inches in each direction, a bit of desert intaglio, vaguely lyre-shaped, with ribs for strings.

Having seen saguaros survive all manner of accidents and assaults, I saw no threat in the little hole, but the first thing I noticed on returning to Phoenix one December was that the whole candelabra was tilting from that spot. Immediately I knew the cactus was doomed. With every rain the pulp takes in as much water as possible, its ribs expanding like bellows. At the first downpour, this one would draw water to its many limbs above the weak point and come crashing down. Judging by the height, it would hit part of the driveway, flattening anything beneath. But the chance of finding anything to flatten was infinitesimal, and in any case, what a memorable obituary. Out of curiosity I even gave it a little push, carefully, through the needles, just above the lyre. I was about as effective as the time I tried the same thing on the Tower of Pisa.

Too quickly I became used to the new shape and didn't even think about the saguaro on a night of pummeling wind and rain, the first winter storm. The next morning I bundled up to retrieve the paper—Arizona was impeaching the hilarious Governor Mecham and I lived for each installment. Halfway out the drive I stopped in my tracks: several tons of highly structured pulp lay at my feet. The rest of the cactus dipped through a small arroyo and rose toward the drive. Here and there, little breaks in the skin showed fresher green. The tip extended two feet over the asphalt. Slightly below it, like a snapped neck, lay a major fracture. I had estimated the saguaro's age to be close to two hundred years, and there was comfort in knowing that—unlike most of Phoenix's recently fallen saguaros—this one had died a quite natural death. The part of me that gave it a push was also sorry not to have watched it go.

Upright, it appeared serene; prostrate, it seemed to writhe. The woodpecker holes facing the sky had filled with water and had become, unexpectedly, miniature potholes. I dipped my finger; the water was icy. I had never walked a fresh saguaro and tried this one: the smooth trunk was a pliant log while the needled branches crackled like a stubble field. Doomed as this saguaro may have been, one of its limbs had put forth a new branch no bigger than a tennis ball. A tight formation, it had landed with its arms side by side like basking crocodiles.

The tip in the drive would have to be dealt with. I tried kicking the cactus aside, but it was firmly attached. I returned with a saw, expecting minor resistance, but the ribs and pulp gave way like pound cake and the tip proved light enough to shove with my foot into the arroyo. As far as I was concerned, that was full cleanup. Most particularly I didn't want that year's gardening crew, looking for inventive chores once they had watered the loquat and trimmed the cassia, to suggest removing the corpus at an hourly rate. It was not practical to explain the weird urge to watch cactus pulp decay, but even professional gardeners understood that the tough woodpecker holes, once freed from the cactus, became "cactus boots." Suitable lacquered cactus boots were sold in Scottsdale souvenir shops. When the gardeners paid their weekly call, I told them to ignore the dead saguaro. "I want to save the boots."

NATURAL ATTRITION was outpaced, alas, by human inadvertence plus the notion that the desert was a 360-degree corridor for human support systems. The children next door, for instance, built a tree house in a paloverde they thought was on their property. They played fortnightly for a season, then the boards fell into an arroyo. The punctured tree turned sallow, then gray, then tumbled into the arroyo next to the fallen tree house, intact to the last twig, looking like an upended root system. One morning the children's father appeared at the door to ask if he could take a truck to his side yard from our driveway to haul out some citrus trimmings. My mother, caught in a bathrobe and without makeup by a neighbor she was meeting for the first time, said certainly: anything to abbreviate the conversation. The truck mangled creosote bushes and dug permanent tracks, and after it left I piled a barrier of stones so no one would take the damage for a spur. The same year, on the other side of the house, the septic tank rudely announced that it had filled, and it had to be dug up and replaced. The disemboweling spread baked clay over an area in which not the least weed subsequently took root.

Whatever its beatings, the desert remained lush enough to crowd the public road by the house, and it seemed appropriate that desert pavement—that slightly blackened mosaic of weathered stones, lichen and small weeds set tight—met real pavement. But the phone company needed to lay line parallel to the road. Here my mother and I became aware of our frail grip on the place, for it was technically owned by Frank's estate and managed by a bank, and we could only watch as a phone company foreman promised a bank representative that the cable crew would respect the desert and revegetate anything they disturbed. They made a surgical cut three feet deep and four inches wide. I was impressed too soon, for next they brought in a backhoe, gouged a trench around the cut and masticated a fifteen-foot strip. Desert pavement that met asphalt had been milled into red earth, raw rocks and chewed plants. Could a utility crew actually revegetate lichen and bursage, and simulate the tiny, anonymous growth that makes the desert look authentic even to someone who doesn't know its particulars?

The bank next learned that the phone company had put the line in the wrong place, but now that it was installed the phone company wanted to leave it and dedicated it as a general utility line. The bank objected, rightly, that it would be exhumed for gas lines and TV cables as soon as it was revegetated, and filed suit to have the phone company move it to where its right-of-way ran—under the road. A compromise was struck whereby the phone company could leave it where it was, had sole use, and had to make good on the revegetation. When I returned the next fall, all I saw was red earth, and I assumed there had been no attempt at all. A month later I stumbled across six clusters of dead twigs in tiny craters: revegetation had consisted of six bursage planted midsummer, watered once, and left to die. Under court order from the bank, the phone company at last hired a nursery to install sixty-three plants—bursage, brittlebush and jojoba—in simulated randomness throughout the red strip, and to water them for a year.

Because of such blows, each time I returned to my mother's house I toured the property in trepidation before I unpacked the car. Had a utility retrenched? Did the dead saguaro survive? Above all, had anyone felled the desert willow? Preserving the willow had become a preoccupation. Native to higher elevations and installed by the previous owners in a garden in back, the desert willow, in late spring, was the property's most beautiful sight, all grace and lacework, a spill of ferny leaves and pale orchidlike blooms. Because it kept the rhythm of its habitat, losing its leaves in October and withholding them until May, I had to explain to each gardening crew that it was not, in fact, a dead tree. One year I returned to find it had been hacked until it looked like an angst-ridden prop from *Waiting for Godot*, and its next attempt to flourish looked more like seaweed on a piling. The gardening crew had remembered my words, knew it was a live tree but trimmed it back because, when it leafed out, it would cast too much shade on the petunias they planned to install. Such was the folly of sinking my own roots where they had so little purchase.

ON THE OTHER HAND, the desert exhilarated through sheer surprise. Once, I stepped out for the morning paper, anticipating more on the gubernatorial recall, and found the first light wrapped in a cold fog through which burned a moon just past full. Two Harris's hawks broke dark and huge into the sky and lit on the tops of nearby saguaros. A third hawk lit on the mailbox like news of disaster. All, including my footsteps, froze, the visible shrunk to this tight tableau while sound, as if through far speakers, reported the roar of commuters on their way into Phoenix. Another dawn I heard, just past the oleanders, the rustle of water. The property's arroyo, which never flowed except in the frenzy of a downpour, was running a clear sweet stream. I followed uphill through neighboring yards to the road, where I found a city truck and two men in jeans: a water main had burst.

"Leave it," I said. "It's great."

"It won't be so great when you turn on the shower and there's nothing there."

"I'll bathe in the stream."

"Not if you want to stay healthy."

This diversion may have further lowered the aquifer under our neighborhood, but it was a pleasure to see water evading its fate in toilets and swimming pools.

The good news was that the desert reinvented itself, endlessly. Clumps of prickly pear would die in the middle and spread at the edge like supernovae. Imported species like cow's tongue prickly pear, from Texas, could be seen claiming arroyos. Creative in its ploys was a smooth-padded prickly pear import, ten feet tall, that had been struck by frost. Dropped pads by the dozens curled beneath it like old snapshots. A few turned into shallow cups that sent a taproot from the middle of the pad straight into the soil. The largest surviving branch of pads leaned over so far it touched the ground, rerooted itself, and sent up a fresh branch like the tail on a check mark. The central pad in the arch of pads, its capstone, was dry as parchment, so that parent and offspring were joined by a link that had actually died.

Just past the oleanders a century plant, which takes a quarter of that time to flower and die, had sent up a twenty-foot stalk. Instead of keeling over, the dead stalk remained upright the following year and turned into a popular bird perch. At last something of the desert could be seen over the oleanders from my bedroom window, and my visitor's count included doves, thrashers, woodpeckers, finches, quail, a cardinal, a kestrel. One night this spindle held a dark star at the top. I got the binoculars to make sure and sharpened the ear tufts of a great horned owl.

The most curious adaptation took place at the site of an old stable in back, torn down when a building inspector complained to my mother about its flapping aluminum roof. After the cement and bare ground beneath it were revealed, I kept my eye on the spot to see what would take root. Nothing, in fact, did take root, any more than it did over the emptied cesspool. Paloverdes still swayed to avoid a roof no longer there, a prickly pear dropped the pads yellowed in the stable's shade, and the cement floor stored the sun's heat. What turned out to be worth watching was the stable's one remaining fixture, a faucet that rose twenty inches from the ground and made a U-turn to a spigot that still poured a full stream when opened. Shut tight, it leaked a large drop of water every few seconds. This water did not vanish into desert air but filled a vessel that someone had placed beneath it years—perhaps decades—back. Fourteen inches long, eleven inches wide, seven inches deep and bright turquoise, this container was filled to the brim in all weather with a variable green mark. Along the top of one side ran a silver bar that said, in tall elegant letters, VEGETABLE CRISPER.

Source of water for the previous owner's horses, this faucet may have doubled as a wildlife oasis ever since a receptacle was placed beneath it, and removal of the barn around it may have only revealed its function. I laid a foam pad behind the paloverdes, which provided a screen, and watched the succession. Ground squirrels stretched on their hind feet and lowered their heads over the rim. Doves, harbingers of water to the desert traveler, perched on the rim and drank, as did finches and those Brits run amok, the starling and the English sparrow. Mockingbirds arrived in pairs, one leading the other, scattering whatever was there first.

Acrobatic types preferred the faucet to the bin. Hornets hovered around the mouth until the arrival of a Gila woodpecker, which perched on the side of the pipe and twisted its bill upward. Facing greater contortions was the curve-billed thrasher, whose bill curves downward, and which had to revolve its neck so that the bill, in fact, curved upward into the falling drop. Perched on this strange metallic tree, birds waited as each fruit ripened, swelling into a globe that, up close, could be seen to catch the saguaros and paloverdes upside down in a tiny jewel. As a drop lost its grip and fell into a bird's bill, cactus and all, the next drop began to swell.

It was, I suppose, an odd household—a woman in her seventies living alone in a rambling house obscured by vegetation in a suburbanized desert, joined seasonally by an adult son who fretted about all that couldn't be seen from the house—dividing their responsibility for property that belonged, legally, to neither of them. My mother, having outlasted two older husbands, at last acquired a younger boyfriend, a jet pilot, who often stayed with us. When she suddenly lost him as well, to cancer, she realized she would no longer have what she called a "beau." "Your mother's a black widow," said an audacious friend. It wasn't that; it was that the line she came from—Landers and Kenworthys of whom I learned little because my mother wasn't interested in family history—had a hard time getting born, but once they existed they were practically unkillable. Relatives of my mother's that I met as a child were already old, had one aging offspring apiece, or none, or didn't marry, but lived into their eighties and nineties. I became my mother's only living blood relative, and while the Berger side reproduced in moderation, I was pleased to be a dead-end Lander or Kenworthy. Given our probable longevity, we could look forward to an infinity of winters in which she pursued gold and I explored the desert. Our interests coincided more closely when she was painting deft watercolors of the landscape I loved, but those were times when she was tending sick husbands, or a sick boyfriend, and art was her only outlet. While there was no injunction against conversing in the house, curiously we talked seriously only when we were off the property—exploring the new restaurants that purported to have invented something called Southwestern cuisine.

SO IT WAS that as the water gathered and fell from the faucet by the vanished stable, each drop holding the world upside down, then letting go, that my mother's heart unaccountably stopped beating. She was only eighty and had been planning to fly alone to Greece in the spring. The ten days in the hospital between the first symptoms and the end were, in the leisurely rhythm of our lives, an instant. I had been planning to stay another four months, and the heirs and the bank allowed me those months "to wind things up." In the aftermath of this inscrutable event, its vacuum, I passed through the oleanders, scotch or coffee in hand, into the desert that now seemed so worn by our presence. How strange it seemed to have arrived as a guest, become a migrant, seen the passing of Frank, of José, of my mother, to be a tenancy's last, and temporary, survivor. From behind the paloverdes I watched doves drink from the crisper, saw the thrasher contort on the faucet, heard the mockingbird peal insolently as ever. Since the property had lost, for me, its human core, it seemed eerie to watch the continuity of it, the sheer sense that nothing had happened.

Because the house now passed to Frank's heirs, two middle-aged daughters from the Midwest who had no intention of moving into it, a FOR SALE sign was swiftly hammered next to the mailbox, with one of the bank's tentacles serving as realtor. Hedges and flower beds were to be maintained for prospective buyers and the desert, as usual, to be ignored. The bank knew its market, for the few prospects scrutinized the oasis in the middle and only asked about the acreage. There was speculation on the bank's part that the house, adequate in its day, was quite obsolete with its low ceilings and rambling floor plan, and a buyer might just want to knock it down and start over. I could only speculate what the razing of one house and the raising of another, more stylish, more fashionably bloated, would do to the crowd at the crisper.

But I had four months to empty the domain within the oleanders, the area I had slept in and ignored. Heaped in drawers, closets and storage areas were two octogenarians' souvenirs of life. Frank's two daughters flew in from Illinois and Minnesota, lightened the load, and left. Bankers, lawyers and realtors filtered through the disarray. Some of my mother's possessions—clothing, accessories—could go to her friends, beyond which loomed an estate sale. More unwieldy were her letters, diaries and more stereo slides than even I had taken. I looked until my eyes fused at the numberless duplicate cruises she took between husbands, with Frank, with her jet pilot, looked until I arrived at my childhood in three dimensions and stopped time. Last and least, I faced my own accretions. They were principally books, relieved by my collection of desert treasures in their bookshelf hollow, furred with dust. Into a burlap bag I had unlittered from the desert, I stashed the leghold trap, the tortoise shell, the pre-Columbian ceramic heads, the burned plate, the cactus boots and related booty, the true detritus of my winters in Phoenix, the desert in a sack.

During these four months I compulsively left doors and windows open, let anything that so desired crawl into the house. I set a card table outside and watched a new crop of cactus wrens explore my typewriter. I lay on the stable's cement floor and felt its stored heat pass through me into the night. One afternoon when I returned to the house, a small red-and-black snake slithered across the kitchen and into a little hole, previously unnoticed, under the carpeting by the doorjamb. I had a few sweaty moments with the reptile book before I determined that it was a banded sand snake, noted for its ability to "swim in loose soil," and not a coral. The snake stuck its head out at various times that afternoon and was never seen again. A near-human screeching roused me one morning, and I stepped outside in time to watch a Gila woodpecker evict a starling from its hole in a saguaro. Shortly thereafter, on a bedroom curtain, I saw the largest hairless spider I have stared at without fear. These incursions, rather than frightening, were reassuring.

The fallen saguaro even handed me a gift. Between its arms, spiders had suspended a mist net stuck with creosote leaves, giving the illusion that the limbs were fingers of land rising from scummy water. I was able to lift a cactus boot from one of these fingers; it was like snapping off a flower, a pomegranate flower in leather, round as a water drop, with a turned-back serrated lip.

Not until two and a half years later, when I reread Willa Cather's *The Professor's House*, did I find some parallel to that four-month limbo. The last chapter of "Tom Outland's Story," her novella within a novel, finds the protagonist, Tom, back on the Blue Mesa, in southwest Colorado, where he and a friend had discovered the cliff dwellings of a vanished civilization. Tom has returned to Washington, D.C., where he failed to interest the federal government in protecting the native heritage at Blue Mesa. Ashamed of his defeat, he finds that the friend, in his absence, had sold the artifacts they found together. The friend actually felt he was acting in Tom's behalf—raising the money to put Tom through college—but Tom accuses him of selling "what belonged to you and me, boys that have no other ancestors to inherit from," and drives his friend away, never to find him again. Realizing too late his own part in destroying a friendship that had been at the core of his emotional life, seeing the first defilement of a civilization that had been preserved intact for centuries, Tom remains on Blue Mesa for the summer. One would expect a season of grief amid this double ruin, but Tom finds, to paraphrase Cather, that for the first time the mesa comes together as a whole in his understanding, that he is simplified into a great happiness: that instead of losing everything, he has found everything. In his most self-damning moment, Tom calls himself "frightened at my own heartlessness."

While I had always considered "Tom Outland's Story" the single greatest fiction about the American West, its last chapter had put me off. How could Cather's appealing character, in the face of human betrayal and natural despoliation, experience such exaltation? Then I reread it after my own mother's death in a shock of self-recognition. A battered five-acre spread within the smog zone of Phoenix was scarcely Tom's Blue Mesa, nor could my dealings with bankers, lawyers, realtors, heirs of Frank and friends of my mother compare with his solitude. My mother's relatively quick, clean passing, after harmonious seasons, spared me the estrangement of Tom's broken friendship. Yet I felt on the property—sure to be further blighted just as Mesa Verde, on which Cather's Blue Mesa was based, was to become an overburdened national park—a fullness, a strange rootedness without attachments. I watched, alert but passive, letting the outside invade the interior, glad for the snake under the carpet. I even leveled at myself, unaware I was soon to reread it in Cather, the word *heartless*. How had Cather known this unreasonable truth, and what truth was it? Was it the sureness of something coming to an end, allowing you to embrace it without restraint? Inadequate, that is as close as I can come.

BUT THE FOUR-MONTH IDYLL "to wind things up" had stored up a climatic fright. I had invited Tom—not Cather's fiction but my own best friend in Phoenix—along with his wife, eight-year-old son, and son's friend to what I had naively billed as a housecooling party, at which they could select items they wanted before an estate sale to be held after I left. Because of an unseasonably hot winter, there had been grass fires already that spring, and I wasn't surprised when one of the boys said you could see a fire in back. I thought of fetching binoculars, then went to look first. Binoculars were unnecessary, for the fire had reached the crisper and was advancing toward the house. I called to Tom's wife, who punched 911, while Tom strung hoses together and ran them to the field. After these years of drift, these suspended four months, was I to wind things up with a conflagration? The air was almost still, but a slight breeze blew crosswise to the house rather than toward it, and Tom had the flames checked by the time the fire department, with three engines and a dozen volunteers, arrived minutes later. Men and machines drenched the area until it stopped smoking, and the event was over as offhandedly as it began. "Now you can have a fire sale instead of an estate sale," remarked Tom, re-coiling the hose. The fire had started in the classic manner: the eight-year-olds had been experimenting with matches from the house, had tried to stamp out their success, and then had run to the house yelling that flames had erupted out of nowhere. Damage to property amounted to some charred fencing. The fire trucks entered where our neighbor had hauled out his citrus clippings, mashing the small barrier I had erected and compacting most of the soil between our house and the next. Several supernovae of prickly pear had burned to extinction and a half-acre of creosote and bursage lay reduced to ash.

I look back on the twelve years of my mother's occupancy of those acres and see that our intention to leave the desert alone resulted, unwittingly, in loss after loss, simply by our being there. The desert, equally unwittingly, had given and given in return: to my mother, a beautiful setting and occasional subject for painting; to me, companionship, anxiety and four months of what I decided, at the time, was heartlessness. The day after the fire I lay behind the paloverdes as doves dipped placidly into the water, mockingbirds scattered the finches, and thrashers craned from the faucet to catch the drops whose inverted world was as coherent as the one I watched from. Nothing, as usual, had happened. In spite of a central loss for me and many losses for the desert, life went on with its business and looked the other way. While I had no thought for Willa Cather at the time, I did think of the last line of a poem I had by heart. "Comfort that does not comprehend," said Edna St. Vincent Millay of the teeming indifference that receives our griefs, giving us strength from dedication that passes us by. It is hard to imagine why such irrelevance helps. It is simply invigorating to be surrounded by creatures that drink and squawk and reroot and decline to care.

Ultimately, there was no way I could help caring, and I only regretted all that escaped notice in the five compromised acres I explored as best I could. In the future I would prefer to be comforted by deserts that are wilder, less abused by myself, and if speech is necessary, perhaps instead of English it could be Spanish, a language raucous as the desert birds. But because this frayed remnant saw me through so much, it will keep replenishing itself through some crack in my attention, nourishing the next people who plant themselves, willfully, in its heart.

THE DRAWERS OF NIGHTSTANDS are filled with hexes against the long dark—a small cross, a book of sayings, a bottle of Valium. For reasons unclear to me, I keep a piece of litter I found under a cactus outside Tucson. I was staying in one of those transition zones where fresh houses breach the desert. My hostess was the developer, a woman who built custom homes—living in one while she supervised the next—until she had designed and inhabited all the houses on a little lane named for herself. It was June 1974, and the temperature was 115. Bored with the air-conditioning, stunned outside, I wandered between the lady's constructions poking at the small.

Otherwise I never would have spotted a scrap so bland and so dense. I reached carefully between the barbs of taller cholla, tweezering it out between thumb and forefinger. I unfolded it once, then again. An inch-and-a-half square unfurled, it was a

Fernando
and Marisela

portrait of a girl against a neutral backdrop, snapped in a cheap studio or perhaps a machine. In her late teens, with full but sad features, she gazed into the lens with moist dark eyes, black lashes, black eyebrows and dyed blond hair. Though the photo was in black and white, you could tell she had one of those bleach jobs that turns dark hair reddish and leaves it murky at the roots. On the other side, in schoolgirl cursive, she had written in Spanish, "Fernando, though you are far away, don't feel alone, for there is one who remembers and will wait for you always. Marisela, Nogales, Sonora. April 17, 1972."

The desert is known for keeping the most fragile objects intact for years. Dated two years back, the photo might have spent its life under the cholla. But two seasons of winter drizzle and two of summer thunderstorms had not turned the paper brittle, nor had two years of burning sun yellowed a corner of the back. The photograph, so charged with unknown lives, had barely preceded me.

But had it been lost or thrown away? The photo gallery in one's pocket seems one more tense of a Spanish verb, and Latin wallets resemble souvenir albums with money in the binding. Marisela's snapshot would have fit neatly in a plastic leaf, and perhaps it had. Yet it had been halved and quartered so that her face was disfigured by the crosshairs of folds as if by a rifle sight, leaving the tiny quadrangle more unwieldy than before. Marisela hadn't been lost; she had been freshly and consciously discarded.

Though you are far away . . . Were all of Marisela's friends dyeing their hair that year, or did she do it just for Fernando? She presumably gave him her picture before he headed to find work in a land where the girls were blond and radiant. When he was far away, surrounded by golden Americans, the photo would remind him that he had a blond girlfriend back home.

The Yankified glamour falsified Marisela's own beauty, but her dewy black eyes held their ground with perfect honesty, perfect desperation.

Far away . . . Yet Tucson is not far; it is a quick and cheap bus ride back to Nogales, a day's excursion. Did Fernando go back to see Marisela? Surely at first. But two years is a long time for a young man tasting the novelties of another country. If she tried to hold him with those pleading moist eyes, he would only have felt trapped and resentful, less inclined to bus himself into the past. If he showed up less often, she would turn icy, then accusative. He might easily drop out of her life, not even think of her for months. One hot spring day, working construction for a lady who built custom homes, he weeded through his wallet during a cigarette break, and ran across this embarrassing back number, this phony blonde who was two years and one language late. Perhaps there was a quick stab of regret, but you couldn't be sentimental forever.

Marisela, it is more than a decade since a passing gringo, stunned by the heat, rescued your photo from beneath a cactus. You were right to let you hair grow dark, to embark on adulthood, to forget the worthless Fernando. After high school your friends married and began families, or became shopgirls, or sold themselves into the streets to Fernando's new cronies from across the border. Nogales is not a town where jilted girlfriends pine by the casement, nor were you the Lady of Shalott. Fernando had doubtless pursued the construction dollar and begun a family with another person, probably not blond. He no longer works for the lady who built custom homes, for she has died, the cactus she left between her constructions has filled with other homes, and her name is kept fresh only by a street sign. The desert is less and less able to keep what we throw away, and your photo barely preceded the bulldozer.

But if you ever feel alone in your new life as a mother, a salesperson, a streetwalker, remember that there is someone far north of Nogales, far north of Tucson, who is unaccountably haunted by your eyes, and who keeps your photograph within reach for solace in the night.

WHEN I READ THAT the Magellan orbiter had sent back infrared photos confirming that mountains on Venus were higher than those on Earth, I hopped in my van and drove south of the little town of Florence, Arizona, to ask my friend Cactus Pete whether he felt vindicated. I had to wait for his coughing fit to stop.

"I was merely thirty years ahead of them," he snapped in his quick, rasping voice. "Back in 1962 I read that some scientists in Tucson were making a geophysical map of Venus. That's just when Kennedy wanted all that money to go to the moon. I took my own map of Venus and asked to compare it with theirs. They laughed and said, 'You show mountains.' I said, 'That's because there *is* mountains.' These guys all had billy goat whiskers, you know, very important. I thanked them for their time and left. Now they're spending more millions

Cactus Pete

to prove what I've already got. I don't even know where I put Venus. It's rolled up around here somewhere." The years had not unscrambled Pete's brain, and I was glad to find him still alive.

Pete had been a loose thread in my life since the early seventies, when I first explored Arizona as an adult. In the course of trying every road in the state, I took the old highway between Phoenix and Tucson. Interstate 10 siphoned off traffic, turning the former artery into a country lane where mallow blooming in every conceivable shade crowded the shoulders. South of Florence, as fields gave way to saguaros, I came upon a knot of buildings blistering behind a wall. A small water tower under wooden scaffolding hung over saguaros dense enough to suggest a cactus garden. A sign said RANCHO SOLEDAD—Ranch of Solitude—and didn't indicate whether it was public or private. As I pulled in, jackrabbits zigzagged in front of my car, the sun shining through their ears. A family of quail wound its way into the underbrush, orioles flashed from the paloverdes, doves exploded in all directions. I felt I had burst into a wildlife sanctuary.

I parked and looked for someone to tell me to leave. There was no one to tell me anything. I proceeded between a pair of long, low buildings with evenly spaced doors that suggested living units. Between them was a pool of bougainvillea leaves. Random small buildings sprawled to the side, their cement blocks painted to resemble adobe. Agave, barrel cactus, ocotillo, aloe vera, cholla and prickly pear, including strains from other locales, were clustered with a density nature reserves for rain forests. Around me chattered finches, woodpeckers, quail thrashers and cactus wrens. Toward the north, where I had come from, the profile of the Superstition Mountains suggested the *Super Chief*, the train that my father—already retired when

I was growing up—took downtown three days a week as a "consulting associate." Brimming with associations, Rancho Soledad looked as if someone had tried to reduce the whole Sonoran Desert, with parts of other deserts, into a single garden. My heart was beating wildly: would it be possible, somehow, to *move into* this place?

As speculation ran wild, I found myself being stared at by an old man who had emerged from behind my car. His mouth was a ruled line. Slight, bespectacled, pencil and Kleenex stuck in his pocket, jeans rolled over his boots, he looked like a professor gone to seed. Not knowing what to say, I blurted, "Are there any rooms for rent?"

"You kidding? This place isn't open to the public anymore." I realized there were no teeth to give his mouth definition.

"OK if I look around?"

"Suit yourself. I'll show you what there is." The place had been built in the thirties as an obscure spa for Easterners bitten by the desert. It had changed hands a number of times. Parts had remained rentable to various degrees, other parts disintegrated. Its future was even more obscure than its past, for it was now owned by an elderly woman in Minnesota who was in the care of nurses and—the old man was sure—of lawyers who were conniving to take the place away from her. She had asked him to caretake the place. More as a favor than for money, he had done so for a number of years.

While he didn't encourage conversation, neither did he fend it off, and I asked how he had wound up here. "From Philadelphia. I had scar tissue in my lung and was given a year and a half to live. That was in 1928. I came to Phoenix and ran into a salesman who was traveling the state. He took me through here, said, 'This is the area, Pete. Why don't you homestead it?' I said, 'I think I will.' I went back to Phoenix and took out papers. I made up my mind I was going to get better or the hell with it. I'm sixty-eight years old and I'm still here."

Years of sun and the loss of teeth made Pete look older than he was, but the story of Easterners who were given up for dead, moved to Arizona and lived to extreme old age was a familiar one: my father made the attempt. Already sixty when I was born, on his second marriage, he had smoked Lucky Strikes almost since they hit the market. To grow up was to watch the deterioration of my father's lungs. Winters in suburban Chicago left him gasping. Because he was retired, because I was young and mostly because rules were looser, my parents simply pulled me out of school for months at a time and we headed south— directly, or by southwest—looking for air to breathe. Cigarettes, not climate, were my father's unraveling, and because he smoked wherever we went, every heaven was a mirage. My mother caught our passage in watercolor and I saw the world. And the best of the world I saw was thirty miles northwest of Rancho Soledad.

In the late forties and early fifties, the air around Phoenix was still pure enough that doctors were telling pulmonary patients to go there rather than to stay away, and many others at the dude ranch had breathing problems. People who coughed like my father were called "Arizona canaries." While my father worked crossword puzzles by the pool, smoked and attempted to breathe, and my mother was wielding her paintbrushes and golf clubs, I discovered the desert. In Illinois, birds built nests; here they gouged holes in pillars of pulp called saguaros. The ears of rabbits were so thin you could see light through fur and flesh. Families of quail wound through the shrubbery like electric trains, lizards vanished into crevices, and roadrunners' legs were as blurred as hummingbirds' wings. And after it rained, the pungency of the creosote bush stirred your lungs with an ache to be just where you were.

I was often the only child on the premises, but there was nothing stern about adult life that revolved around horseback rides, chuck wagon dinners, square dancing, costume parties concocted by a social hostess, drives on the Apache Trail and shopping expeditions to Nogales. Adobe cottages around patios were filled with people who stayed weeks, or months, and became a family. A seasoned hotel brat, I played the piano in the lobby, won at bingo and beat businessmen at gin rummy. Wanting desperately for my mother to share the desert, I lured her up Camelback Mountain, where we got trapped over a dropoff. My adventure was her trauma, and after that she seldom ventured beyond sight of her clubs or her easel. One morning all guests were told to report to the pool at eleven for an important surprise. We arrived to find that bathing beauties of a sort never before seen at mature Jokake Inn had been placed in strategic positions. Photographers shot the aquatic mob scene from every angle, and the next September we received an *Arizona Highways* with the three of us on the inside cover—my father working a crossword in a formal gray suit, my mother in a two-piece bathing suit, my pallor stretched on a pad—swamped by glamorous extras. Desert dude life was fulfillment: why bother with anything else?

Time, as I later learned, cures paradise, and when I got to high school, my parents were not allowed to pull me out for a ten-week stretch. My father ultimately went cold turkey on tobacco, but the damage was done and he didn't live to see my college graduation. My mother married another Arizona-bound Chicagoan and wound up living—as if coached by her paints—only a few miles from where we had first seen the desert. I visited a couple of times over Christmas, then spent a season with a friend near downtown Phoenix. When my mother was widowed a second time, I simply moved in with her every winter. Perhaps the creosote had chafed my lungs the way tobacco had my father's, for the desert had become my addiction.

Phoenix, however, was overcoming the desert. The so-called bedroom community where my mother lived became a corridor community, as if it had been kicked into the hall. Winter temperature inversions trapped the particulates, blurring and sometimes annihilating the horizon. Spores from introduced plants gave people lung problems they didn't arrive with, and Arizona canaries were told to try one of the smaller towns, maybe Prescott or Wickenburg to the north. Camelback Mountain bristled with electroguarded homes, and the homespun Jokake Inn had been replaced by a five-star Xanadu, pitched by the eminent swindler Charles Keating. Reaching the desert meant threading a battlefield of streets ripped up for widening, sewer lines being trenched, vegetation being bulldozed, and phone, power and TV cables being slung or buried to service bermed layouts of townhouses, villas and ranchettes among the groundwater lagoons. Slowed but unstopped, I fought my way through to the cactus. And one day I drove past a sign that said RANCHO SOLEDAD, straight into my childhood.

SINCE THERE WAS no way to move in, let alone to make a rash offer to buy it, there was nothing left but to drop in now and then, to stroll through the dilapidation, and to talk, increasingly, with the opinionated Pete. "The city fathers of Florence didn't know what they were doing. They tore down a bunch of old territorial buildings because they were ashamed of them, when they could have restored them and turned Florence into another Santa Fe. That Senator McFarland was the crookedest politician we ever had. The interstate should have come through here, but McFarland bought land outside of Casa Grande, got the highway to go through there, and made his bundle. So what does Florence do? It turns the old hospital into a historical museum and names it for McFarland. That's Florence City Hall for you."

When Pete didn't show up at the eroding spa, I tracked him to his ramshackle house to the south. The old lady in Minnesota hung on from year to year, attended by nurses, plotted against by lawyers. At last she died, but the estate was in probate and the fate of Rancho Soledad became no clearer.

After paying my respects to the ranch and to Pete, I usually completed the visit by eating in the restaurant just to the south of Pete's house, a place with its own peculiarities. There was nothing odd in its desperate swing between cheap steaks and Mexican fare, a pattern for marginal restaurants all over the West. Its rambling, low-ceilinged rooms were classically roadhouse, but the building's south end, over the bar, was a half-cylinder like a tin can split lengthwise and placed round side up, its rondure sagging in parody of a covered wagon. Beyond the cylinder, at the acute angle formed by the highway and a back road to the cotton-farming town of Coolidge, stood a freestanding white tower of four cubes, each smaller than the one beneath it, exaggerating its modest height. Door locked, lower windows boarded, upper windows giving on the darkness, it was a Babel for sparrows. Between this assortment and the road, visible for miles either way, stood a pair of date palms like spiky feather dusters. The whole lineup—from Rancho Soledad through Pete's house, the restaurant and palms to the tower—mutated from nostalgia to dementia. This, it seemed to say, is what can happen to civilization in the desert.

While Rancho Soledad was in probate, I was browsing the Southwestern section of a used-book store in Santa Fe and was caught, as if by a saguaro spine, by the spine of a book that read *Cactus Forest*, by Zephine Humphrey. No mention of Rancho Soledad appeared on the jacket, but I was so sure the place lurked inside that I paid $7.50 for what was marked as a "First Edition" even though I suspected it was the only edition, and whisked it to my motel room.

The tale, published in 1938, begins in Vermont, where the author's husband is laid up with sciatica and all remedies fail until the sixth doctor commands: "Arizona. Lie in that dry sunlight all winter and keep away from doctors." On their drive west, a waiter in Lordsburg, New Mexico, informs them that he, too, had sciatica and wasn't cured until he went east. Tucson, where they plan to settle, is abrasive and full of tourists. They head north over roads I had explored in my Arizona wanderings, until they find just what they're looking for "five miles below Florence"—the precise location of Rancho Soledad.

Congratulating myself on my intuition, I next read that they settle into an adobe cottage made by "a young Philadelphian who, eight years before, had gone to Arizona for his health," and whose name was Erwin Peters. I knew from Pete's mailbox, officially, that he was E. A. Peters, assumed his nickname came from his last name and that "Cactus" was added by Florence neighbors. Erwin, therefore, was the young Cactus Pete, and his place was something called Cactus Forest Ranch—a half dozen one-room housekeeping cottages hidden from one another in the desert. Forsaking her usual humor and invoking the sublimity used to embalm Frank Lloyd Wright, Humphrey says of the place: "Never was variety more skillfully employed to embroider unity; never did unity more serenely triumph over variety, using it for purposes of complete integrity." The Humphreys watch Erwin build a new cottage. Erwin's mother, embarrassed by her German accent, presides over the Peters living room, a gathering place for guests. The image of restored health, Erwin treats himself with an undisclosed kind of "animal oil," as well as a "mineral mud" from "elsewhere in Arizona." One morning, as if to prove a point, Erwin appears at the Humphreys' door "coughing and wheezing," tells them a cold is no problem, and returns from Coolidge at four that afternoon "completely cured by one chiropractic treatment." The Humphreys had always scorned chiropractic, but after hearing Erwin rave about the Coolidge chiropractor, Christopher Humphrey goes to a Phoenix osteopath recommended by a friend in Vermont. The osteopath evens Christopher's legs, he lies in the desert sun, and halfway through their stay he steps out of his sciatica "as if it had been an old pair of slippers."

Cactus Forest Ranch? And no mention of Rancho Soledad? The next time I dropped in on Pete I was full of questions, and I asked him about the book.

"Zephine? Oh, yeah, nice lady. Come here several winters. She signed a copy to me. I've got it somewhere with my maps. I've just mapped Jupiter. Know that red spot? Turns out to be a premonitory."

I didn't understand a thing after the part about Zephine and was determined to pursue the matter of the cottages. "Pete, what's Cactus Forest Ranch?"

"That's a few guest places I built across the road. It was sometime in the thirties. Lots of the guests were millionaires from the East. They told me they liked it better than being at home, that it was really living. There was an aide to General Pershing who stayed with his bodyguard. Also that guy Juilliard who built the music school in New York. His wife was always worried about his hump. They weren't all rich." Zephine had mentioned an archaeologist, a woman who broke her writer's block and finished a book in two months, a pair of businesswomen and a rodeo rider. "I also put up a six-room adobe house for ourselves. My mother came out and stayed awhile. They put manure instead of straw in the adobe, the termites in the manure ate all the woodwork, and we had to pull the house down. The cottages fell down on their own. Know that black hole they found? There's interesting minerals in it."

What I really wanted to pursue was why Zephine hadn't mentioned Rancho Soledad, since it would seem to have been there at the time, and she even mentioned (misspelling it) Jokake Inn, forty miles away. But I could see Pete's mind was elsewhere, so I said, "Do you have some kind of telescope?"

"Don't need one. I've mapped all the planets. There's mountains on Venus but nobody will believe me. I'm part of the Earth's surface. I do it by magnetism. If it wasn't for magnetism, nobody'd be alive."

"You mean you just draw the surface of the planets freehand? You don't use an instrument at all?"

"I use my doodlebug."

"Your which?"

"Gizmo I made myself. I'll show it to you sometime."

Sometime was not now, and I left finding the little string of buildings more cryptic than ever.

When the will was settled, the resort didn't wind up in the hands of lawyers, but it was uncertain whether it would be offered for sale or bought by the county for a rest home. On the possibility that it might actually come on the market, I asked Pete to take me inside the buildings. The largest of them, where the owner had lived and provided a common room for guests, would have made a perfect desert home by itself, and I was particularly impressed by some hand-carved doors I was unaware of. There was a root cellar I'd never noticed, a gap in the weeds that proved to be a shuffleboard court, and an organ pipe cactus from Peru that Pete pointed out. More eye-catching, alas, were the crumbling guest quarters surrounding a cracked, empty pool. The water table had dropped and the well had to be drilled another twenty-five feet. The plumbing and wiring were shot and had to be redone. Looking at the matter coldly, I could see I was trying to recapture my grade school idyll under Camelback Mountain. The reality was that patching, buttressing, supervising and restoring would be thrust upon someone who really didn't like to handle anything messier than a dictionary. You couldn't be a hotel brat and also run the hotel.

I had by no means abandoned the area and had developed a fondness for Florence itself, an unassuming town with a couple of good Mexican restaurants and a tiny downtown that got a minor tidying for a minor film with James Garner and Sally Field called *Murphy's Romance*. While its surviving territorial buildings were on the National Register, its most appealing structure was an eclectic 1891 brick courthouse with mansard roof, dormers, and circular windows. Zephine, who had higher standards, called it "a sheer architectural monstrosity." Because there was no money to buy a clock for the polygonal cupola, dials had been painted in all four directions, reading seventeen minutes to twelve. There was something winsome about a town where it was always quarter-to-lunch. In the notion that Florence might not be a bad place to live outside of, I dropped into a real estate agency, explaining that I was interested in living in unpopulated desert—did they have anything to show me? "Hop in," said a realtor who had just arrived from a boom in Alaska.

We cruised in his sedan past Rancho Soledad, south toward Tucson. "What do you see as the future of Florence?" I asked.

"Frustrating. The whole town is owned by a couple of families who don't want the place to grow. The state pen is the only real business around here, and the people who run it don't even live in Florence because there's no place for them. They commute from Mesa, Phoenix, even Tucson. We'd like to get a Safeway, but a chain won't come unless there's a certain number of people, and we're below the minimum. These families own all the little businesses, and they don't want the competition."

We pulled onto a dirt road, bottomed out in some potholes and crossed a cattle guard. "What I'm showing you is a strip of private land that just came on the market. It's got BLM land front and back, so you'd never have any neighbors except on the side, and these are five-acre parcels. They're prime and they'll be going fast." We walked several of them; cactus soared, paloverdes hummed with bees, and house finches chattered excitedly. Realtor's hype aside, these lots deserved to go fast. But if I didn't want to patch, how could I conceive of constructing? Scavenger that I am, I was looking for the perfect shell to fill like a hermit crab.

On the ride back, the salesman, thinking he might have put me off with the backwardness of Florence, said, "Well, even if the town doesn't want to improve, we could still get the world's largest jetport."

"The *what*?"

"The aviation facilities in Phoenix and Tucson are both too small, and this would be something really future-oriented, right in the middle."

"Isn't it a little far from each place?"

"They're talking light rail in both directions, but the

airport wouldn't just be for passengers. Federal Express is very interested. This could be the shipping hub for the *whole Southwest*."

We rode the rest of the way in silence. I took the realtor's card, then drove back fast to Rancho Soledad. "Do you know anything about a plan to put a jetport in Florence?" I asked Pete.

"Sure," he said, his cavernous mouth beaming for the first time. "Been talking about it for years. This time we might actually get it."

"Where would it be in relation to Rancho Soledad?"

"We're standing on it."

"Wouldn't you lose everything here?"

"Lose? Think what I could leave my kids!"

Around this time, two Florence-related incidents pursued me to Phoenix. One was that Pete and I had adjacent letters in *The Arizona Republic*. Mine protested the overcutting of forests; Pete's promoted the jetport. Since Pete never actually learned my name, only I could relish the irony.

The other incident involved a pre-concert drink with a friend my concert-mate wanted me to meet. For some reason the conversation turned to Florence. "It's a wonderful place," said the friend's friend.

"Really?" I asked eagerly. "I'm thinking of buying some land there and possibly building."

"If you do," he said, "I'll have to give you a letter of introduction to a friend of mine there, William Weaver, the opera commentator, who also translates Italo Calvino. He's got a villa and is surrounded by servants. He's terrifically bright and great fun."

How odd that someone so sophisticated as William Weaver should live in Florence! Still, with interesting company added to cactus and Mexican food, perhaps I should make use of that realtor's card . . . About halfway through the concert, as the Phoenix Symphony was sawing through some Schumann, it suddenly burst into my head that all through the conversation my friend's friend was talking about Florence, *Italy*, while I, monomaniacally, was talking about Florence, Arizona.

Having floated Glen Canyon just before it was dammed, driven the Baja Peninsula before the road was paved, lived on Cannery Row before it became a boutique, and in Aspen before it appeared in the *National Enquirer*, was I now about to put down roots in Florence before the jetport? For someone whose sense of identity derived from surroundings rather than a nuclear family, emotional survival was increasingly a lesson in nonattachment, and on learning of the jetport, my interest in Florence, as the locus of my future, crested and waned. I let years pass between visits. Did Rancho Soledad go through a rest-home phase? I got little information from Pete. "I don't think it's working out for the county. There's a few people there paying rent, but I don't have to mess with it anymore. These big outfits make me mad. I just wrote to the School of Health at New York University. I told them I'd like to get some blood samples of AIDS. I think I've got the answer. They said the government wouldn't let them ship anything like that. Instead, they sent me a report this thick. I threw it in the fire."

WHILE I NO LONGER thought of becoming Pete's neighbor, the inscrutability of his corner picked at me. It seems I'd overreacted to the specter of the jetport, for the Phoenix papers never mentioned it until a politician, fishing for rural votes, resurrected it in a speech and prompted an editorial in the usually development-minded *Arizona Republic*, saying they assumed that particular imbecility had been laid to rest. Less momentous questions still nagged: How did a desert homesteader map the planets? What was the significance of the square tower? What was the cure for AIDS? On reading that the space probe had discovered mountains on Venus of the sort Pete had mapped in his back room, I drove to Florence in a mood for answers. After a three-year absence, that would depend, of course, on finding Pete alive.

I pulled into Rancho Soledad, past a FOR SALE sign. A man in his sixties was sitting on the porch of one of the smaller buildings. "Is Pete here?" I asked.

"Who?"

"Cactus Pete. Erwin A. Peters."

"Oh, sure. He's living across the road, in the house under the water tower."

I now knew there were two water towers in the neighborhood, as well as the restaurant tower. Pete's current house was as ramshackle as the other but set back from the highway, more private. I called "Pete," let myself in the gate, and knocked at the door. Soon there was Pete peering through the screen, the sky behind my head glittering in his glasses. "Yeah?"

I explained that I saw that NASA had confirmed what he'd said about the mountains on Venus, had been interested in various things he'd told me over the years and would like to ask a few questions if that was all right.

"Sure, come in." He held the door open. "Do I know you? You have to excuse me. I've had a few strokes."

"I'm the guy who kept asking about Rancho Soledad."

"Oh, yeah," he said, though I wasn't sure he made the connection, any more than I'd ever been convinced that he remembered me from visit to visit. He'd looked older than his age when I first met him but hadn't changed much since and now merely looked his age. "Sit down. If you'd come five minutes earlier, you'd have missed me. Just came back from the chiropractor in Coolidge. Just got over a cold, but I can't seem to shake this cough. Mountains on Venus?" He dissolved into a spasm of coughing and wheezing that ended in gasps for breath. As he told me how he'd first mapped the Venusian ranges back in 1962, I stifled the urge to ask if he'd just seen the same Coolidge chiropractor who had cured his cold in 1937, as reported by Zephine Humphrey. I could see that he was more bent than before, and though the day seemed warm to me, he was bundled in a shapeless sweater leaching some shade of faded.

"If this isn't a good time . . . ," I began.

"Let me make a fire." He stooped to a pile of sticks, laid them in an iron stove angled in the corner and lit them.

"What kind of wood is that?"

"Just dead creosote, OK for some quick heat. I get it with a wheelbarrow. When you're eighty-six, you gotta keep busy with something. I found out how to take the radiation out of those power lines, to make them safe. I wrote and told them, but they didn't even answer. They'd rather take government money to bury the lines, which won't solve the problem. At least I got a letter back from Mrs. Bush, so I'm that far ahead."

I was always impressed that Pete, unknown and marooned in the desert, never shrank from the world's stage. Since he had plunged in, I didn't hesitate. "How do you get out the radiation? The same way you map the planets?"

"With the doodlebug."

"Can I *see* the doodlebug?"

"Haven't I ever shown it to you?" He seemed genuinely surprised and headed to the back room. In his hand when he returned was a small spring with a rubber handle on one end and a plastic cone on the other. "Hold your hand out." The doodlebug wagged puppyishly in front of me, seemingly impelled by a motion in his wrist. "You're full of nuclear, but I've taken the nuclear out of that chair. Sit down." I sank into a gray armchair with a towel draped over the back. "Now get up." He held the doodlebug in front of me. It was as still as his wrist. "See? The nuclear's gone that quick. Let's sit down."

After we settled, I said, "I still don't understand how the doodlebug works."

"I got a bunch of them. They're easy to make. All you need is a spring and some uranium."

"That's what's in the tip? Uranium ore?"

"Exactly. Uranium ore."

"So the force is atomic."

"No, it's magnetic. Way I figure, I'm in the negative return circuit. I pick the magnetism up through the doodlebug when it comes back from the sun. Your college boys won't recognize me because I'm not one of them. I had two and a half years of high school."

"How did you get the idea to do this?"

"Mining. I mapped mining properties. If I wanted to find a mineral, I'd make a map, then go pick the mineral up. I made the first doodlebug fifty years ago. That's how I got onto planets, doing mining."

"Is it like dowsing?"

"Sort of. The doodlebug finds things underground. I started a vertical map of this place years ago. The ocean's been in here seventeen times. I dug a hole and put a pair of crossbeams on each level, to show where the oceans were, but when I was almost finished some kids pulled the cord and they all came out. Kids are terrible. But when you correlate the seventeen oceans with the oil, it fits. Some of the cactus around here look like coral, and I know the sea is where the desert plants come from."

I remembered that the desert reminded Frank Lloyd Wright of the ocean partly because the staghorn cactus suggested coral, but what was metaphor for Wright was evolutionary evidence for Pete. "So you struck oil?" I said.

"I found oil just across the road, eight hundred feet down. A guy from Coolidge raised the money to drill from a company back in Massachusetts. My boy and I worked on that well for nine months, and as soon as we hit oil the company shut it off. They wouldn't pay me for it, and we didn't have the money to work it ourselves. The mining companies only want your information. They tell you they're not interested, then they move in after you've gone. I wouldn't let them do that to me, so all I've got are some samples. I'll get one."

I was grateful for a moment to collect stray thoughts and inspect Pete's living quarters. The furniture was like Pete's sweater, faded and shapeless, with towels over the backs of chairs and a blanket over the sofa. Taped to the wall were pictures of children, a portrait of Barry Goldwater, and clippings about solar energy and Arizona political scandals. Across two walls was a collage of objects, mostly iron, arrayed with an eye to design: horseshoes, spikes, canteens, ice tongs, a mining pan, ax blades and, wired to the wall, a green bottle whose red label rebounded from pre-Jokake childhood. I jumped up to make sure, and there was the red devil prancing in front of a massive hotel. It was Pluto Water from French Lick, Indiana, where my parents took me when I was seven, when my father could still breathe. We had stayed in a grandiose resort built around a spring that smelled like rotten eggs and was bottled, my mother said, "for people who can't go to the bathroom." I was reading the fine print on the label, lost in the nostalgia of first travel, when Pete reappeared with a half-gallon jar. "It's Pennsylvania oil, but we hit it in water." Oil and water oozed in layers in a way that reminded me of lava lamps, lights of gaudy, heated, writhing liquids people stared at in the sixties—nostalgia of later travel. "All the oil around here is mixed with water."

"If this area has so much oil, why didn't the big companies ever come in?"

"Phillips drilled an exploration well down the road in Tom Mix Wash, and Mobil drilled farther on, but they didn't do it right. Hell, I could have told them, but they didn't ask me. There's surface oil right on the property."

"Can I see it?"

"Come on." We proceeded outside, and Pete deposited the oil sample on a table where another two dozen jars stood like sun tea. He grabbed two plastic cups, and we passed through old stoves and tires into the cactus. "This stuff belonged to my partner. He died a while back. Isn't this air wonderful?"

The air was soft and delicious. "Pete, has the desert changed much since you got here?"

"There's a lot less growing now. See how there's no little plants?" It was true; the bursage, brittlebush and varied grasses were missing; between the saguaro and barrel cactus was packed, bare earth. "The county made a diversion in a wash a couple of miles from here and never figured where the water would wind up. Every time it rains, the water floods through my property and washes away the topsoil." It suddenly struck me how much Pete *did* make sense: the predation of mining companies and the ignorance of the county were perfectly plausible. At this point I spotted some black lumps on the ground ahead and thought, "Surely not." To my stupefaction, Pete bent down and peeled off what I recognized as black cryptogam, a lichen-and-algae community that holds the desert soil in place. He handed it to me and said, "What did I tell you? Oil, right on the surface! Look at it." I held it close and saw the tiny plants, like hairs of black velvet. Before I could think of what to say, he put the cryptogam in one of the plastic cups and said, "Come, I'll give you more proof. I've also got paraffin."

"Wax?"

"Wax, whatever. It's associated with oil." We started back toward the house. He set down the cup of cryptogam and descended with the other cup into a tight arroyo, raising his arms away from some catclaw acacia. The Superstition Mountains, floating over his head through the cactus, seemed aptly named. He bent down and picked some moss off one bank. He started to climb out, slipped, grabbed a creosote branch and pulled himself back up. "You get this old, you lose your balance," he grumbled.

We continued toward the house and suddenly he stopped, breathing hard. "I feel knocked out," he gasped. "I shouldn't exercise after a cold. There's probably an earthquake going on somewhere. No matter where in the world it hits, I feel it. You'll probably read about it in the next couple of days."

He breathed easier and returned through the gate. He set plastic cups on the table and said, "Let's check these out. If it's oil, it should fizz." He opened an unmarked brown bottle; the fumes reached him before he could pour, and he began to choke. When his breath steadied, he filled the cup.

"What's the liquid?" I asked.

"Hydrochloric acid." Each cup looked full of mud and neither fizzed. "Maybe it will take a while," he said. "Let's go in and sit down."

I was relieved he had survived our excursion and felt the need to change the subject. "Pete, did you build Rancho Soledad?"

"No, somebody else built it after I got here."

"Zephine didn't mention it." Pete had arrived in 1928, eight years before Zephine had arrived with her sciatic husband; either she had written around it or Rancho Soledad was built after 1936.

"I can't remember now what happened when, but I homesteaded six hundred forty acres and built a lot of other stuff, like the Chuck Wagon Restaurant and that tower."

I had struck oil. "What was the tower for?"

"It was to advertise my gas station. Saguaro Petroleum was the Gulf agent in Phoenix and they said, 'Peters, we like your location.' I said, 'What does that do for me?' They said, 'If we can put in a five-thousand-gallon tank, we'll give you a nine percent margin.' I had a windmill on the corner, but who looks at a windmill? I took off the blades and the tail, encased the rest in plaster, and painted it white. The Saguaro Petroleum people outlined the whole thing in red and green neon. By the time it was finished, you could see the thing for fifteen or twenty miles either way. It was about the *only* thing you could see."

I had pictured the tower's four cubes deliberately shrinking on the way up to make it look taller. "You mean there's a windmill inside that tower still? Why is it built to look like four boxes?"

Pete looked surprised. "A windmill slants toward the top. If you're going to make a tower, you're got to square it off."

"Do you let people go in?"

"I never fixed it up on the inside or let anyone in for fear there'd be an accident. It was just for show. The only person but me who went up it was a convict who escaped from the pen in Florence. He stopped for water at the well at Rancho Soledad, was about to be caught, broke into the tower, climbed up and begged for mercy out of the top window."

"And the round part of the restaurant, next to the tower, was meant to look like a chuck wagon?"

"Originally it was the *whole* restaurant. It doesn't look like a chuck wagon now because some people I sold it to added all that square stuff that's much bigger. I made the wagon by bending reinforcing rods at different radiuses, stretching chicken wire over the rods, then pouring plaster over the chicken wire. The Quonset hut came out soon after I opened the restaurant, and I think that's where they got the idea. My best customers weren't from the road. They were those rich people from the East I rented cottages to. They liked nothing better than to go across the road and have breakfast in their pajamas and bathrobe—it was something they couldn't do at home. They loved it. You were looking at that bottle a little while ago, that Pluto Water."

I didn't know I'd been caught. "When I was little, my parents took me where that stuff comes from."

"That was my novelty drink. I gave it away free, and also to minors who wanted alcohol. One kid got mad because he lost his girlfriend when she got diarrhea. The Chuck Wagon lost him his date, but it got me my wife. The superintendent of the hospital in Florence came in one night with two nurses. I saw one of them and said, 'That's it!' I married her. We had a pretty good life together. Then she broke her back. That's when I started the clinic."

"Besides the cottages and restaurant and gas station, you had a clinic?"

"The clinic is the only reason I ever wanted money. A long time ago I was looking for perlite with a partner out of Superior, and he told me his wife had breast cancer. After we found the perlite with the doodlebug, I asked if I could use the doodlebug to take the cancer out of his wife. In ninety days I had her in remission."

"I don't see the connection."

"Magnetic. Same as I took the nuclear out of you when you sat in my chair this morning. So when my wife broke her back, and was gradually paralyzed, I set up a clinic in the back of the Chuck Wagon, complete with two osteopaths, phones and equipment. I taught them what I knew about magnetic and nuclear. They both made enough to move out on me. They took everything I gave them, even the X-ray lab. My wife died after that. That's when I made my mind up that anything I tried to do, I had to do on my own. So before I kick the bucket, the one thing I want to do is get a clinic going."

"A *new* clinic?" Sometimes I found myself repeating to make sure I'd heard right.

"There's a doctor now in Tucson who brings patients to me when he can't do anything for them. I take the radiation out of them so they have a chance to get well. When people get sick, I get answers. They gave five million dollars in New York for a report saying that everyone exposed to power lines was going to die from cancer. Hell, I've got the cure, but they're educated and won't listen to someone like me. And they won't send the AIDS blood. So you see the politics."

"And after your wife died," I said, returning to an easier thread, "you never remarried?"

"Not actually. When my partner died, he left a nice little woman. When I was driving back from Wyoming once, something told me to drop in on her in Glendale, outside of Phoenix. I had a feeling. She came to the door and said, 'Oh, Pete, you're just in time. Take me to Florence.' I said, 'Get your duds together,' and she lived with me for ten years. Never had an argument, never got married, had a good life together, then *she* got sick. I used to put out feed for the quail, and she'd sit all day watching them. So I outlived her, too."

The idiosyncrasy, the complication, the withstanding of loss in this scrap of American road culture, brought my thinking to a halt. To get started again, I summed, "Besides Rancho Soledad, which wasn't yours, there was the restaurant, the gas station, the clinic, the rental cottages, the house with the manure, the tower around the windmill . . ."

"And the amusement park. We had a merry-go-round and a train. It was the adults who really loved to ride the train, especially after a few drinks. I built it for my son. There was a fight in the school bus and he got hit on the head with a book. It knocked him out for a long time and I was afraid of brain damage. I wanted to leave something to support him if he couldn't work. But he turned out OK, and I closed the amusement park the day we took in seventy-five cents. I also have two daughters, and they're OK, too. A lot can happen in sixty-three years."

"Whatever happened, this had to be the biggest thing on the road between Phoenix and Tucson."

"Road?" Pete laughed. "There was no road when I got here, just a dirt track, a so-called military highway from 1889. I worked eighteen years just to get it oiled and the town of Florence wouldn't help me. That's how progressive they are. Everything I ever wanted, Florence was against. I had the Mexicans on my side, and the truck drivers wanted the road through Florence, but Florence was run by the Presbyterian Church." Perhaps he was overcome by the notion of Presbyterians, for suddenly he began to cough uncontrollably, ending in spasms and gasps.

"If the doodlebug can cure cancer and AIDS," I ventured, "can't it do something about that cough?"

"What?"

"Can't the Coolidge chiropractor cure your cough? Or the doodlebug?"

"These colds just go around. Everybody gets them."

While he recovered his breath, I sat, further digesting information. Pete didn't mind the silence, for unless pressed he didn't speak at all. Now and then thoughts demanded to get out, but there was no urgency to voice the transitions. "Pete," I finally said, "where do all your ideas come from?"

"I take a shot of Jim Beam whiskey every night before I go to bed, with some water and sugar so I don't get too much booze. But that's to *stop* thinking. Some nights I can't sleep at all. Things come to me and I get up and work them out. When Mount St. Helens erupted, I put it on paper. I located those missiles in Cuba. Remember those H-bombs that were missing off the coast of Spain? I wrote the Air Force where they were. What's the name of that colored general?"

"Colin Powell."

"Powell. I sent him a map of Hussein's headquarters, not that they'll give it to him. That's why I wrote to Mrs. Bush. I said, I know your husband is too busy with the Persian Gulf deal so I'm writing to you. I also wanted President Bush to know I had the answer to the power lines."

"The radiation?"

"Yeah. To prove to Mrs. Bush that I knew what I was talking about, I sent her a diagram of an atom. It's radium, carbon— Christ, I can't think. I've had some seizures. Anyway, the power companies were on NBC a couple of weeks ago, trying to get the president's OK to move or bury all those lines so they won't cause cancer. Of course they want the government contracts. I could go to each plant and show them what to do instead. There's a hundred twelve companies, and I want forty-five thousand dollars from each one. That's five million."

Suddenly I felt as if I had fit together two remote pieces of a jigsaw. "Isn't five million the amount you said you needed to build a new clinic?"

"That's the one thing I want to do before I die, the one thing I want money for. I can cure people, and I need to pass that on. Let's look at those specimens and see if they're fizzed yet."

The afternoon sun hit us square in the eyes. The mud in the two plastic cups had partially settled, green shading to orange and the top in a way that suggested tomatillo sauce going bad. "See?" he said simply. "It's oil."

It was clearly time to leave, but I had to satisfy one more bit of curiosity. "You know, Pete," I said, "I've never actually seen one of your maps. Could I see Venus?"

"No, you can't see Venus, because I don't know where I've put it. It's the first one I did, and it's way back somewhere. I'll show you something else." We went back to the house, into a small room with a workbench smothered in tools. On the floor, so thick we could barely stand, were supermarket bags filled with large rolls of paper. He pulled a roll out of a bag at random, took it into the living room, and started unfurling it. I took the end and held it until seven feet of paper, three feet wide, stretched with vibrant color between us. "What is it?" I asked.

"Halley's Comet."

Shaped vaguely like a map of Malaya, it was a ragged-edged, intricate mosaic of meshed polygons shaded with colored pencil—a Balkanized, tutti-frutti, hundred-faceted gem cut by a jeweler gone mad. Black lines that burst into wire stars stuck out like spikes from the perimeter. I asked to see more, and Pete showed me two: Uranus and an object called Levy's Comet—named, he said, for a Tucson astronomer who discovered it but wouldn't look at his map. Assuming that the grocery bags held roll after roll of such creations, here was a major collection of original, baroque, beautiful, unwitting folk art. In the guise of a crackpot scientist, here, perhaps, was the Grandma Moses of American abstraction. The sheer complication and scope was impressive. "How do you do it?"

"With the doodlebug. The doodlebug moves around, and wherever it moves I make a line. I just think of some celestial object, put the paper on the workbench, and start."

I couldn't picture doing such intricate and precise work with the gizmo in one hand, and I realized one would have to watch to understand. "What are these spidery lines on the outside?"

"I think they're collectors that absorb the radiation that gives these objects the power to turn."

"Both these comets are angular. I thought comets were round, with tails."

"This is the way they came out. In all the articles they write, comets are ice and goo. But look at all these colors. Every color represents a different mineral. And these are only the important ones. I didn't put in the iron and stuff."

At the top of Halley's Comet was careful writing, upside down. "What does that say?" I asked.

"It's a list of the minerals that correspond to the colors. I've written it upside down so it's harder for people to read if I show it to them, but I'll let you look."

I turned the paper around and read, out loud, "Radium, uranium, mercury, iridium, *caliche*?"

"That's calcium deposit."

I knew very well what caliche was. Caliche, alias hardpan,

was that unyielding layer under the Sonoran Desert that scorned anyone trying to install basements or palm trees. Caliche was the saline, calcified flooring left when lakebeds dried, that mineralized solution that rose from the subsoil through capillary action, to congeal where the hot, ravening air couldn't reach. An inch thick or a yard, it informed anyone who pried beneath that the desert's granular surface is a false bottom. By extension—and what were Pete's maps but extension—caliche was the impenetrable layer of politics, betrayal, survival of loved ones, failure to be taken seriously. Caliche was the Florence Presbyterians and caliche was what filled my father's lungs. Pete had been resisting caliche ever since the doctors gave him a year and a half to live in 1928. Anyone could work down to caliche, but it took a desiccated, sandblown, persecuted, calloused, moonstruck desert rat to find caliche on a comet.

AS MARS WAS ONCE thought to be, Phoenix is crisscrossed by canals. Except for what remains of its desert setting, canals may be Phoenix's most distinguishing feature. Varying little, pooling a personality, they make soft incisions through what surrounds them. As you jockey through traffic dizzied by small businesses and their signs, numbed by miles of ranch homes and convenience stores, your eyes will flicker coolly down what seems an open tunnel of water. Receding parallels of packed desert sand, twenty feet wide, clean of vegetation, frame an even, sky-reflecting flow. Glimpses of joggers and cyclists along the banks indicate that there is still human life without combustion. For all their sterility, the canals command moving water and thus retain more mystery than anything else in the valley. Because they so prominently display what makes a

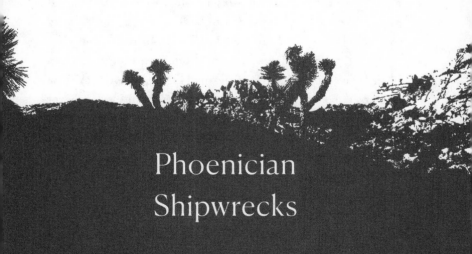

Phoenician
Shipwrecks

desert city possible, it would seem that to get to the bottom of the canals would be to get to the bottom of Phoenix.

Part of the canals' mystique is that some of their routes predate Phoenix by nearly two millennia. Beginning around A.D. 200, Hohokam Indians, using handheld digging tools, moved tons of earth and engineered the largest pre-Columbian irrigation system in the Western Hemisphere. Some 250 miles of canals fanned like tufts of hair from the Salt River, irrigating several thousand acres of corn, squash, beans, pumpkins and cotton. Having reached a population of twenty thousand, the Hohokam abandoned the Salt River Valley around 1400, possibly because they had depleted the soil.

For the next four centuries the drainage cooked in the sun, its canal system choked with the debris of flash floods. The dormancy lasted until just after the Civil War, when gold miners burst into the Arizona Territory. Migrants to the West Coast passed through the valley. U.S. Army forts were established to the northwest at Prescott and Wickenburg, and upstream from Phoenix at Fort McDowell, to fend off Apaches. Miners, migrants, and soldiers all needed to be fed. In 1867 a scheming ex-Confederate soldier named Jack Swilling responded with the Swilling Irrigation and Canal Company. Using Mexican labor, he retrenched many of the old Hohokam canals. Alfalfa for horses and grain for persons soon flowed from the Salt River Valley to the forts. So responsive was the soil that miners and migrants, safe from attack, grabbed shovels and went what was soon called "canal crazy."

The founding of the Swilling Irrigation Company was, in essence, the founding of Phoenix. An American grid of streets was imposed on the snaking, geologically determined weft of canals. Canals bred canals, and Anglo machines were able to tap the Salt River farther upstream than had been possible for the Hohokam. The river's wild floods clearly couldn't be allowed to roar through the reworked water system, returning it to waste, and a canal users' association called the Salt River Project was organized to brake the flow. Private and territorial boosters lobbied for passage of the National Reclamation Act of 1902 and landed a federal grant for what is still the world's tallest masonry dam, eighty miles upstream on the Salt River. Named for a president eager to replumb the West, Roosevelt Dam was completed in 1911, one year before Arizona became a state. It was eventually joined by three more dams on the Salt River and two on the Rio Verde, which meets the Salt just above Phoenix.

The history of Phoenix, from outpost through oasis to elephantiasis, is written in channeled water. With the completion of Granite Reef Dam in 1908, just upstream from Phoenix, it was possible to split the entire flow of the Salt River to either side of the river itself, so that 100 percent was siphoned into man-made canals and zero percent maintained the riverbed. Changing attitudes toward the canals present an oblique but curious record of how America expressed itself on its driest fringe and remind us that, even in the desert, water remains a primary figure for the human unconscious.

THE SALT RIVER PROJECT consolidated a system from canals that farmers and water companies had dug on their own. This system incorporates 151 miles of main canals that deliver water to 880 miles of subsidiary canals, called laterals. From there, it is the prerogative of every recipient, or group of recipients, to take the water through any system they have rigged and to irrigate what they will. As alfalfa, the main original crop, was replaced by citrus groves and then by residential neighborhoods, the delivery points remained exactly where they were. The urbanization of an agricultural area with its irrigation system intact created a genuine novelty: a desert city of canals.

As Phoenix started to expand into its farms and orchards, life became intimate with the flow of water. The riparian zone of the Salt River, to be sure, died at a blow when Granite Reef Dam cut off the flow, but in another sense, the river habitat splintered and fissioned through the canals. The laterals were open ditches with culverts where streets passed over. Shady Fremont cottonwoods, the dominant tree along the Salt River, fanned through the new water system, along with willows and tamarisk. From the twenties through the fifties, when dude ranches were romantic getaways for Easterners who rode horses into the desert, the outdoor life of locals centered on the canals. No one yet had private swimming pools, and in summer, when water still ran cool from the reservoirs, children learned to swim in the canals. Swings hung from cottonwood branches over the water. Arizona's native fish used the system freely, and people fished from bridges and canal banks for bass, crappie and catfish. Eric Bergersen, who later became a fish biologist, remembers a bloom of silverfin shad from Saguaro Lake that poured into the laterals and got stranded during irrigation on the lawns. "They stank for a while, then they became good fertilizer." And where there were roads instead of trees along the bank, people skimmed along the canals on aquaplanes and water skis, holding a rope from a car.

Living with the canals meant accepting the risk of open water. More perilous than the canals were the laterals, where children splashed through the undergrowth and dared one another to swim through culverts that often had no air at all and could be clogged with brush in the middle. Child drownings were a summer staple. When water spilled over a canal bank, flooding a neighborhood so that water covered the baseboard plugs and people worried about electrocution, a friend of mine became a teenage hero by digging a trench in a bank farther down, which the water itself widened on its way back into the system. "Instead of being grateful," he says, "the Salt River Project was mad as hell that I had violated their sacred canal bank." Water skiing at fifty miles per hour in a canal fifty feet wide took skill, and those who veered into the banks came to grief. Neighborhoods considered the canals their social centers, and people accepted the dangers in the same way they tolerated swimming with dead cats, dogs and snakes. Adults staked ropes over the banks to provide sure places to get out, watched over their children and taught them safe swimming. Most of the resorts were beyond the canal system, but Frank Lloyd Wright designed a textile block bridge over the Arizona Canal to harmonize architecturally with his Arizona Biltmore, and the canal-side Ingleside Resort had canoes, a romantic promenade and a waterfall.

Through the end of the fifties, Phoenix grew in leafy, low-keyed neighborhoods. Even when houses took over citrus groves, many of the orange and grapefruit trees were left standing. With the sixties came walled subdivisions full of houses with backyard pools, and the mentality shifted abruptly. Canals were now the murky area over the wall, slightly mysterious and decidedly unsafe. There was a push from mothers, taken up by the newspapers, to cover the laterals because children could drown there, and the laterals disappeared into buried pipes. Canals were literally screened out of people's lives, and the Salt River Project, flowing with opinion, put out messages on the radio and in the schools not to swim in them. As the canals became demonized, people who lived in the immaculate subdivisions threw their trash over the wall into what had been communal playgrounds, and once the canals had become corridors of garbage, there was a clamor from the very perpetrators to clean them up.

The Salt River Project had never been happy to see water mandated for agricultural, municipal and industrial uses being transpired into the sky by cottonwood trees. The political climate was ripe for defoliation. Cottonwoods, tamarisk and willows along the banks were felled and plants were cleared. Annuals such as weeds and wildflowers were poisoned. Service roads were elevated on either side of the banks, and the porous interiors of the canals were lined with gunite, a brew of sand, cement and water sprayed three inches thick onto a wire mesh. People who fished during the purification remember that when there were cottonwoods on one side and gunite banks on the other, all the fish were under the cottonwoods. In 1973, the Salt River Project inserted steps painted yellow every fifty yards along the canal banks, but only as emergency exits for people who fell in. By the time the devegetation and lining of the canals were complete, the man-made but luxuriant meanders that had softened and socialized Phoenix reflected only gunite, phone poles, utility wires and sky.

EVEN AS THE CANALS were sanitized and agricultural lands were diced for tract housing, water continued to arrive at the delivery points, creating a system unique to any American city. A citizen whose home sits in a former alfalfa field or citrus grove may sign up for water to flood his yard. Water arrives every fourteen days from April through September and every twenty-eight days the rest of the year. Deliveries are measured in time, and a typical fifth-of-an-acre lot will take forty-five minutes of water, or 27,000 gallons. Water is rotated through the network of laterals on a twenty-four-hour basis, and each lateral services several blocks of a city. Recipients are responsible for opening the valves in their yards when their turn comes, whether it is during the day or in the middle of the night. They must also maintain any ditches, gates, valves or berms on their properties.

By this subterranean means, the ghost of the Salt River still holds a neighborhood together or pulls it apart. Blocks scheduled for night deliveries will sometimes keep vigil at someone's house over coffee or drinks to supervise a smooth passage from yard to yard. Those unable or unwilling to twist their valves at odd hours may hire zanjeros, whose function is to turn valves on cue and watch that water doesn't spill over. Spillage is a serious offense, for water does not merely moisten the ground; it steeps in the yard, swamps the grass, turns flower beds to gruel. Homeowners who let their allotment escape have been responsible for up to 40,000 gallons of rogue water that can destroy a neighbor's den, chew up the streets, and divert cars into each other. Letting water run wild is a misdemeanor, and as a Salt River Project brochure observes, "Once water is ordered, it can not be sent back." The Salt River Project's official obligation ends at the delivery point, and they try to make neighborhoods themselves deal with local problems, such as a neighbor who doesn't clean his ditch. They have, however, been forced to hire field representatives who try to get neighbors to cooperate and who have authority to close the headgate if a neighborhood just lets the water run. One neighborhood was about to be cut off when the flooding was traced to a tied monkey who had no diversion but the valve.

Even after sterilization, the system itself remained strange enough to spark incident. A bar friend of mine was deluged with Esther Williams memorabilia when it was reported that he had driven home after last call, rolled out of his car and landed facedown during irrigation night. He might have drowned on his front lawn if his roommate hadn't heard the splash.

In another neighborhood a canal-loving friend, who nearly died as a child when a lateral pulled him under a sluice gate, was throwing rocks into a gunite-lined canal with buddies at the age of fifteen. He spotted what looked like "a shoulder and a cowlick" drifting slowly in the middle of the water. Unsure of the object, he chucked a rock, hit the cowlick and heard a thud so dull he was sure it was a man or a mannequin. He ran home and interrupted a card game between his mother and his uncle with the story. The uncle, half convinced, called the police. By the time they caught up with the object, it had gone through a lock at Central Avenue and resurfaced as a fully clothed adult male. The body was still mid-canal, and police and firemen tried to reach him from the bank with hooks. Tom's uncle, disgusted with squeamishness in uniform, plunged in and dragged the body to shore. Dressed in a suit, tie and wingtip shoes, the victim sported an expensive watch and an unrecognizable face. Because the year was 1971, the zenith of the mob-related Arizona land-fraud murders, Tom was sure that the man had been done in and dumped. The police report stated that the deceased, overdressed as he may have been, was repairing his car on a service road when he fell backward into the canal, and his death was declared an accident.

Such larks are the exception, and most of today's adventure is suffered by those who unwittingly drive through neighborhoods toward a canal to find that streets come irrationally to a dead end, hook into residential circles, or double back on themselves as grid turns to labyrinth. Peering into those labyrinths from the canal banks, one sees that the backyards are furnished with endless permutations of swing sets, patio furniture, oleander hedges, barbecues and small pools. The neatness and lack of eccentricity suggest that Phoenicians have become a passive lot, content to tend their gardens, unconcerned that their river has been diverted into most undiverting canals.

THERE ARE, HOWEVER, active Phoenicians who have looked urban dissolution in the face and seen the canals as potential deliverance. They have built-in constituency in the many citizens who walk, jog or bike along the canal banks, both for exercise and for nonmotorized transportation, braving vistas of cinder blocks, employee parking, dumpsters, and windowless office backs. In the fourteen contiguous communities serviced by the Salt River Project canals, a battalion of civic groups has proposed a transformation of the canals to include landscaping, drinking fountains, pocket parks, equestrian trails, waterside rests, pedestrian bridges, islands, underpasses, illumination, signs to tell you what street you're crossing, pedestrian-activated traffic lights, integration with canal-side housing projects, public art, decorative paving, a mini-railroad, restoration of an old waterfall, and call boxes for emergencies. Renovated canals are seen as a way of linking greater Phoenix while each community projects its own identity. Scottsdale would specialize in outdoor cafés and shops fronting the canal. Gilbert would feature a farmers' market. It seems apt that Sharon Southerland, president of the Metropolitan Canal Alliance, which coordinates the planning groups, bonded with the unreformed canals as a child, nearly drowning when she tried to swim through a pipe.

Southerland sees the canal projects as a link to the city's origins. Archaeological studies, she says, keep raising the percentage of the main canal routes that follow those dug by the

Hohokam, a figure now approaching 70 percent. Modern Phoenix is made possible by the canals: they are drinking water, irrigation, life. With grant money from various communities and the National Endowment for the Arts, the College of Archaeology and Design at Arizona State University has come up with guidelines that have been endorsed, sometimes in extravagant language, by public officials. Said the mayor of Scottsdale, "I think the canal banks can be almost as great an attraction as the ocean in San Diego, even in August." Said the assistant professor of architecture who is spearheading the plan, "We want to create a memorable image so that people think of us like other memorable cities throughout the world, such as Paris and Vienna." Most observers agree that it will take more than well-trimmed water to turn Phoenix into Paris or Vienna, and a more reasonable—and interesting—perspective is offered by Cindy Ashton, also of the Metropolitan Canal Alliance. "Someday people are going to fly into Phoenix and there will be green lines winding through town. It's an *aerial* identity that people will want to explore on the ground." Southerland is quick to add, "But we're looking at it not as a tourist attraction, but as a way to improve our own lives."

Beyond agreeing on the details and then paying for them, a major impediment is the Salt River Project's system of service roads. Says Southerland, "You can't do anything on the banks that gets in the way of trucks going by. The canals are also corridors for electric lines. Near the water, for instance, we can have planters but not rooted trees. We're looking at hydroseeding and native grass right up to the edge. That's what it looks like in the spring now, until the Salt River Project poisons the vegetation." While Southerland claims a good working relationship with the Salt River Project, she also bluntly stated what I had suspected. "The Salt River Project uses us as a buffer with the public. It's good PR."

To see how citizen greening of the canals sat with the Salt River Project, I left the Metropolitan Canal Alliance, which was camped in the temporary headquarters of the Phoenix Junior League, upstairs in a shopping mall, and negotiated traffic to a sprawling office building set in acres of parking. The Salt River Project does not just run one valley's canal system. It is part owner of various coal-fired power plants, including the Navajo Generating Plant, which had just been ordered to stop smogging the Grand Canyon; it generates hydroelectric power on the Salt, Verde and Colorado rivers; it partially owns the controversial Palo Verde Nuclear Generating Station; and it is the third-largest power utility in the United States. Meeting me by appointment were Paul Cherrington and John Egan, respectively manager of water transmission and superintendent of media relations.

Cherrington and Egan led me through a warren of polished halls to a sanctum I had hoped to see, the control room of the canal system. Theater-like, its banks of manned computers faced a curved wall of screens that showed the canal networks north and south of the Salt River, along with a screen called a water log, which scrolls through the canals' measuring devices and can report the precise amount of water at any given point. Cherrington explained that the Salt River Project's zanjeros in the field take orders from farmers, residents and water treatment plants, then a water master determines each day how much water needs to be drawn from the storage dams and in what ratio it should be divided at Granite Reef Dam into the system's two parts. "The control system is getting very automated. Every gate out there is telemetered back to the computer terminals here." He bent to an unoccupied terminal and began pressing keys. "We can open a gate just by putting the cursor here and pushing this button on the left."

"During the summer thunderstorms, this is a very interesting place to be," said John Egan. "We have people getting information from the U.S. Weather Service radar, which happens to be just down the hall. There are water masters taking floodwater in and water masters keeping the canals from overflowing. It's a real madhouse." A quite unmad calm marked our visit, but it was a calm in which one could dispatch a smart bomb.

Once we had retreated to a generic office, I asked Cherrington and Egan their opinion of canal reformation. "I'm chairman of the Salt River Project's Canal Multiple Use Coordinating Center, which entertains all the various proposals," said Cherrington. "You have to realize, of course, that our job is to deliver water, which belongs to the users, not the Salt River Project, and part of our job is keeping the canals clean." Growth of vegetation in the canals, he explained, had been a problem since their inception, because the combination of silt and sunlight grows algae, moss and weeds that can use up to half the water and choke the channels themselves. Canals were historically cleaned by stopping the water and clearing the bottom with horse-drawn scrapers. The first canals to have roads on both sides were dredged, full, with ship chains hauled by trucks. Eventually chemicals were introduced, which are more effective on plant life but tended to worry people who received their drinking water from one of the canals' seven water treatment plants. The thirty-day dry-up was instituted by Phoenix. In this operation the canals, in rotation, are emptied and the Salt River Project gets in, sprays gunite and scours them.

Two recent additions to the cleaning process may aid the forces of transformation. One is the telescoop, a long-armed robot that can clean the canal from one side, freeing the other side to be vegetated. But ever more uptown is the white amur, a vegetarian carp from Asia, commercially grown in Arkansas. Weighing seven pounds when released, an amur can eat its weight in vegetable matter daily and in fifteen years may grow up to five feet long and weigh seventy-five pounds. Arizona's ravaged native fish are protected in that only sterile amurs are released, and amur-proof grates keep them within the system. Fifteen thousand amurs were dumped into the canals between 1989 and 1992, and they have proved the cheapest and safest canal cleaner yet—though dry-ups, machines, and chemicals downstream from the treatment plants are still used in changing combinations.

Now that I was up to speed on canal cleaning, Cherrington addressed my question. "We have a fifty-foot right-of-way from the highline of the canal, but we need only fifteen or twenty feet for equipment. We have agreed, in certain cases, to give up one side of the canal, and will give up both sides if the city in question will pick up the tab for maintaining that part of the canal. We resist trees within fifteen feet of the canal, and we resist boats. But the trend now is toward attractive canals, and there's pressure to build things like the San Antonio River Walk."

I found it curious that both the Metropolitan Canal Alliance and the Salt River Project referred to the precedent set by the popular River Walk in San Antonio, Texas—and both agreed that River Walk, though admirable, was puny and artificial in comparison. River Walk was only a few blocks long and water was diverted to it strictly for effect. The Phoenix canals, by comparison, were 181 miles long if you included an extra 50 miles of canals that remained outside the Salt River Project system. That was 362 miles of canal bank: no other American city had anything like it.

I left the Salt River Project tallying the phases the Phoenix canal system had gone through: Hohokam routes; canal consolidation under the Salt River Project; canals as social centers teeming with natural growth; sterilization and ban on public recreation following the advent of walled subdivisions; now plans to convert the canals to highly structured, mulitple-use greenbelts. The revival of recreation at the canals was hardly a return to the era of swings hung over swimming holes from cottonwood limbs, although many people planning the reconstituted canals lived their childhoods during that period and might unconsciously be trying to reproduce it. The new focus on the canals was rehabilitation by master plan, with every planter positioned, every café table in conformity with rules of access, every bypath checked for liability, every inspiration—however lovely—thrashed out by committee. It was hard to be spontaneous in the age of litigation. The improvements, if brought to fruition, would vastly enliven the waterways that cross the Salt River Valley so bald and alike. And in continuing to reflect America in controlled water, the plans project, unavoidably, the age of shopping malls, of political compromise, of safety, of bond elections, and of social correctness and urban design.

Of course, all the assorted forms of canal craziness overlook what Phoenix and the Salt River Valley might have been if the water—even part of the water—had been left in the river. It was, to be sure, the Hohokam, and not the Anglo, who dipped the first straw, but the Hohokam lacked the storage dams to gain total control. If enough water had been left to maintain riverbanks of cottonwood and willow, with habitat for tanagers, otters and herons, the Salt River might have made a luxuriant focus for a romantic city of canals. But total control, once gained, was exercised, reducing the riverbed to a waste of gravel operations and blowing trash. A proposal to restore a section of the river, again with highly structured landscaping, was voted down, primarily because it seemed to tax all of Greater Phoenix to benefit one area. During the spectacular flood years of 1978 and 1980, when record rains and snowmelt funneled water even five storage dams couldn't handle, water poured through the bed of the Salt River like lava, severing all but two bridges, undermining the interstate, infuriating commuters and bringing smiles to the faces of river lovers. While the water was unable to rouse a long-dead ecosystem, it was viscerally thrilling to watch that raw, sinewed power even while stalled bumper to bumper on a gridlocked bridge. It hinted at the Phoenix that might have been.

Phoenicians have accepted for generations the theft of their river, usually without a thought, and the few who take offense vent their spleen on the agency with the power, the Salt River Project. One such person—the one who incurred the wrath of the Salt River Project by breaching one of their canal banks as a teenager, and who returns the sentiment—is Tim Means, who later gave up managership of a Phoenix Jack in the Box to become a guide on the Colorado River. I once had the pleasure of touring the Phoenix Zoo with Tim. At one point the displays parted to reveal, across Mill Avenue, the corporate headquarters of the Salt River Project. As if reading a sign in front of a cage, Tim extemporized, "Salt River Project. *Projectio Fluminis Salarius*. Endemic to Arizona, where it is the most

dangerous predator. Exhibits beaverlike compulsion to im-
pound moving water. Favored prey species include wild rivers
and tax dollars. DO NOT FEED."

MY OWN CANAL MADNESS was the idée fixe that to get to the
bottom of the canals was to get to the bottom of Phoenix—an
act best accomplished during dry-up. Because the canals are
public, and it is a global vice to dispose of unwanted objects in
moving water, for eleven months each year the canal is fed a
rich diet that is exposed when the sections are dried for repairs.
As with ski resorts, where locals walk under the chairlifts when
the snow melts to see what has fallen out of suspended pockets, Phoenix scavengers prowl the canals for booty when the
sluice gates shut. Reported finds have included vending machines, refrigerators, tires, chassis, couches, money, jewelry,
guns, needles and, for the first to arrive, edible fish. In answer
to my question, John Egan said, "Yes, we find six to ten bodies
a year, but Phoenix is not the murder capital of the United
States." The canal had been empty for two weeks when I made
my foray, so I had missed the good stuff, but it was still an opportunity to test my notion.

I was first overcome by the stench. It had rained in the
night and the canal had a stagnant marine smell, as if the sea
had been locked in a closet. The name of the original canal
company—Swilling—floated to mind. The bottom was not the
smoother surface I expected; rocky here and muddy there, it
was grained with what looked like tide ripples between bits of
broken mirror, hubcaps and plastic bags. The canal banks had
the look of plain dirt, with weeds at the waterline, so that I was
unsure whether I was looking at disintegrating gunite or a
stretch of canal that had never been lined at all. As I forced my-

self to continue through what seemed a festering hospital corridor, I could see by the prints of people and dogs and the treads of bicycles that many adventurers had preceded me. Dominating all other refuse, the principal landmarks of that anticlimactic stroll were shopping carts sprawling on their sides, on their ends, even upside down, at regular intervals. Dripping with algae that bleached like Spanish moss, stuck with shredded plastic, flecked with Styrofoam, they loomed in that shrunken perspective with the grandeur of shipwrecks.

Just when my nostrils had reached their limit, my eye was caught by a frantic, swarming movement on the canal bottom in the distance. I raised the binoculars I carry in the most unpromising locales and found, to my astonishment, a flock of Audubon's warblers—the first I'd seen in metropolitan Phoenix—hopping, darting, veering off and back, stabbing greedily at nourishment I couldn't imagine. That banquet was the image that stuck when I tried to get to the bottom of Phoenix: the hunger of creatures, gorgeous in the individual, feeding in the most straitened circumstance.

ONE WINTER IN LA PAZ, I moved into a particularly vibrant and chaotic neighborhood, renting an A-frame with palm-thatch extensions before it was supplemented with a one-room, five-sided guesthouse. That architectural hybrid perfectly reflected an outlying barrio of open fields, housing for phosphate miners, an acupuncture clinic, walled-in private houses, a gutted bus, a storage yard for phone cables, and a collapsing kiln tended by an owl. My landlady, Maria Eugenia, a compressed, energetic woman from Puebla who was always incubating five plans at once, told me that the original A was no more than inward-leaning pieces of sheet metal that shaded a rabbit hutch when she bought the property. She converted it to living quarters, installed a loft, added a thatch to shade the front and projected another thatch in back over a kitchen-and-bath addition. Doing construction herself gave her such

Curse of the
Adorers

unexpected clarity that at the end of each day she wrote out her thoughts—the present and its projections—most of which still seemed valid several years later. "Did you know that Jung built a house and experienced the same kind of focus?" she asked. "When I read that, I recognized it, because I, too, felt very rooted in myself."

Maria Eugenia had moved with her five-year-old daughter into a trailer in the front yard, renting the A-frame to help an older daughter, now eighteen, through school in Switzerland. Calls from Geneva and Berlin, Milan and Hong Kong, converged on her tiny quarters. When I said that I felt bad about living in the larger house while she lived in the trailer, she said, "Don't. I actually prefer living in a space so small there's no room for mistakes. Stay in the A-frame or I'll rent it to someone else."

With bookshelves over the john and fishnet thrown rakishly over the palm thatch to keep it from blowing off, the A-frame reflected Maria Eugenia's improvisational nature. Eight steep steps led to a loft with a bed, above which, at the apex of the A, a child's cot perched like a crow's nest. Here, propped on pillows to counter the inward-leaning walls, in a stew of binoculars, legal pads, pencils, coffee cup and bird book—seeing but unseen behind a triangle of tinted window—I read, wrote and spied on a half-secret world in back.

Beyond a small field, once plowed and now running to seed, spread a panorama of beehives, scattered work buildings, a chicken coop, a weather station, a palm-thatch pigpen and a string of goats that were herded from one end of the spread to the other. Commanding the center was the dormitory complex of El Convento de las Adoratrices—the Convent of the Adorers—behind which rose the cupola and cross of the convent's only public building, a chapel that fronted a street on the far side. Lark sparrows enlivened the field, a lone cattle egret befriended the pigsty, and the first time I glimpsed scarlet I thought it was a cardinal. Emerging from the trees surrounding the convent door, it was a nun. A black wimple spilled down her back, a white robe swept her ankles, and a brilliant red scapular glittered from shoulders to sandals, fore and aft. The splendor of this tricolored plumage made spying on the nunnery less like voyeurism, more like bird-watching.

Within a few days I knew the outdoor routine. Every morning, just after dawn, a stout man in a T-shirt that said "Bass Lake" ambled through the back entrance, sometimes with his teenage son. Greeting him on their way to the goat pen were two or three elderly nuns whose tenderness seemed almost allegorical as they bent to nursing goats that tugged ravenously at the nipples of baby bottles of milk. Punctually at seven, a young nun in a pale blue uniform emerged from the convent with what looked from a distance like musical staff paper and took readings from the weather station. Another young nun in blue gathered eggs in the coop. Bass Lake, helped by his son and a few stray nuns, herded the goats across the open driveway from the pen to the fenced field.

Already I had favorite goats: the black one twice as large as the others and the strange brown-and-white one that looked like a fawn emerging from a sheep. As the day progressed, younger nuns in blue uniforms hung washing. Bass Lake tended bees, directed irrigation water here and there by rearranging dirt with a spade, repaired fences. Sometime mid-morning the oldest nun would stroll out with a walking stick, coming to a full stop to confer with the sister who walked with her—not for secrecy, I surmised, but because she was deaf. The nuns never left the premises in less than full regalia, whether driving their blue camper, a curry-colored station wagon or a sporty red coupe. A driver's education car showed up late afternoon, and I imagined the instructor telling the assembled, in a turn that would work as well in Spanish, "The foundation is good driving habits, so I want you to begin by trimming your right sleeves . . ." Two clotheslines threaded the palms, with black, white and red habit parts blowing aside to reveal white nightgowns and long white underwear on the line behind.

One Saturday morning I saw a half-dozen neighbors gathered around a reddish object suspended from a beam in front of the convent. The binoculars revealed it to be a goat, tied by its back hooves and skinned. Bass Lake stood chatting with a coffee cup in one hand and a machete in the other. Now and then he handed the coffee cup to his son, hacked off some goat and tossed it into a turquoise plastic bin. When the neighbors left, Bass Lake dismantled the goat in earnest, handing the head to the boy, who took it like the ace of hearts to the convent door—thence, I liked to imagine, to a satanic soup, or perhaps the indoor dogs.

A nun emerged and spoke to father and son. They repaired to the pen for another goat, which they dragged toward the beam with a rope as it bawled and dug its heels. Having sometimes thrived on goat until my floss ran out, I forced myself to follow a scene the vegetarian reader is advised to skip. The men wound the rope around the goat's torso and back legs, pulled tight, and suspended the animal upside down from the beam. It continued to thrash and attempt to lift its spine, even after the man slit its throat. The man rapped the goat on all sides with a stick, to speed the draining of the blood or to free the hide of dust. When they were halfway through the skinning, a nun emerged with a plate of cookies under a plastic wrap, which she handed to the boy. He carried the cookies to his house, beyond my field of vision, while the man finished the skinning and tossed the hide in a wheelbarrow—which, I now saw, also held the hide of the first goat. The boy returned for a lesson in goat carving. Two nuns emerged with the indoor dogs, a pair of small spaniels, on leads. The man tossed them scraps. Nuns, dogs and men all left, and again I wrongly assumed the scene was over, for Bass Lake returned with yet another goat—a martyrdom I skipped except to note that it was the morning's last.

When I relayed this scene to Maria Eugenia, she reported that the neighborhood ran with speculation that the nuns were selling eggs, honey and goat meat at the market without a permit. Competitors at the market, it was said, didn't complain "because they are afraid the devil will come after them." A few years back neighbors did protest about the pigs because of the smell and the city took them away, but the nuns kept a few piglets and bred them back.

Interested in seeing these urban ranchers up close, when the bells rang for mass the day after the goat slaughter, I slipped into the chapel that was their one public building. The rectangle of a room floated in robin's-egg blue, and light from clerestories mixed with neon tubing to create a bright aquarium. A large bas-relief shell in deeper blues behind the altar framed a gilded globe, with the Americas facing forward. Two guitarists noodled random chords as worshipers straggled in. Circulating through the aquarium were eight nuns, their scarlet dulled by the neon, and what I had taken to be a large key with looping chain on the flank of one of the nuns—perhaps the church key itself—proved to be a rosary with cross. A priest in a green tunic convened the ceremony by saying that we would pray for the same recently departed that we did last week—and I realized that church regulations required that this exclusively female religious domain import a male to conduct its most important rites. Mass itself was relieved by two lively songs for which the congregation stood and sang to guitar accompaniment, one a *huapango* beat, the other a *paso doble*. Below the altar stood a small crucifix whose Christ hung so low from the crosspiece that the Y of his arms suggested a suspended goat.

THE PANTOMIME of the convent might suggest that the neighborhood was quiet, and indeed it was calmer than the older, denser parts of La Paz. Much reduced were radios blaring ranchera music, revving motors, repair shops that worked at all hours. Several mornings a week a woman and a man took turns at a microphone yelling *Un! Dos! Un! Dos! Uno! Uno! Un! Dos!* to a school gym class, sometimes followed by band practice, at a school several blocks away. Cars in first gear, with speakers so loud that voices were nearly unintelligible, cruised the streets raving of discounts or all-star shows or proclaiming, "Five people hover agonizingly between life and death after hitting a cow last night at kilometer thirty-four—read about it in *El Madrugador* [The Early Riser], your newspaper," its exhaust distributing a blue cloud like a pall of sleaze. Next door lived a blacksmith who worked amid showering sparks in his backyard, and his hammer on iron rang unpredictably through the A-frame. But none of these distractions had the thought-obliterating persistence of the convent's three outdoor dogs. The nuns' dorm was clouded in trees, but through the binoculars I could make out a shepherd mix and two lesser hounds pacing a mysterious shelf just below the second story. Barking pealed from the convent as if from a band shell.

Sounds withstood by day become intolerable at night, and the usual prescription for insomnia—plugs and pills—was no match for the convent. Maria Eugenia, equally incensed, decided to put a stop to all noise after bedtime. She persuaded the blacksmith to take in for the night his schnauzer with a yap like high-pitched vomiting. Enraged at drag racing on the highway several blocks off, she phoned the police to say that if they didn't stop it, she was going to the waterfront to commit an act she couldn't predict. Within half an hour the combustion ceased. A week later, ranchera music from distant public speakers two-stepped all night, spinning and spinning the same few chords like a hamster on a treadmill. Maria Eugenia called to complain. Nothing happened. Two hours later she called back. The police reported that they were getting an awful lot of calls from one woman. Next morning Maria Eugenia called talk radio to complain on the air of the noise *and* the uncooperative police. "I would like," she told me, "to proclaim my property a private anarchy." I admired the sentiment, but that seemed to me already the status of every lot in La Paz.

I left town for two weeks, didn't think once of noise in the barrio, and returned to find that Maria Eugenia had had a rough time: the phone and water had both been accidentally cut off, she had gotten sick, and as she lay with a rebellious stomach, the convent dogs had raved nonstop. She confronted Bass Lake and demanded that the dogs be taken off the roof that broadcast their barking. "You will have to take that up with the Mother Superior," he said, "and the Mother Superior is away."

For Maria Eugenia, it was war. Neighbors knew, she said, that Bass Lake had put out laced meat without warning local dog owners, alleging that stray dogs were attacking the convent's chickens and goats. Dog poisoning, it must be said, is not considered as heinous in Mexico as it is in the United States. Once a year the city of La Paz warned all residents to keep their pets inside, then picked up all strays and dispatched them. La Paz was free from rabies, but from feces to roving packs, the dogs created hazards. "We love animals," Alejandrina the veterinarian told me, "but we don't carry on about them like you Americans. They *are* replaceable." I realized their ubiquity when I went to throw something in a trash barrel at the local supermarket, shrank from a stirring inside, then approached to find an entire submerged dog licking a meat tray. But replaceable or not, the acupuncturist and the blacksmith had both lost dogs to the convent, and both were livid. Did the nuns actually *know* what their employee was doing? I asked Maria Eugenia. Maybe, maybe not, she said, but how could the convent, as an entity, eliminate other people's dogs and not take responsibility for its own? She plotted a letter to the police, with a copy to the convent, detailing the barking, the dog poisoning, and throwing in, as an attention-getter, the resurrection of the illegal pigs. All she needed, she said, was a night to sleep on it.

It was a sleep she didn't get, for during the night her trailer was invaded by bees from the convent hives. Fearing they might be killer bees, she grabbed her daughter and fled to her camper truck, there to be serenaded by the yowlers on the roof. At dawn she ventured into the trailer and found more than a hundred bees had entered through a vent in the hot-water heater. *"Es la maldición de las Adoratrices,"* she cracked. It's the curse of the Adorers.

Because her word processor was broken, Maria Eugenia took her handwritten letter to a public secretary to type, then brought it to me to cosign. Addressed to the police department, the text read, "It is important that you know that the Colonia Puesta del Sol has been bothered by noise problems such as high-volume radios during the hours of rest, as well as dogs on roofs. We ask your support and assistance in ensuring the peace and quiet of this barrio." Copies were specifically directed to the acupuncturist, the trailer park out on the highway, and the convent, with others for general distribution. I learned for the first time that our neighborhood had a name—roughly Sunset Suburb—but was disappointed, as if by a fizzled plot, that the text was so mild. "What about poisoned dogs and illegal pigs?" I asked. "What about confronting the Mother Superior with what her employee is doing?"

"That's for later. We begin with this, and if it doesn't get results, we escalate."

Maria Eugenia spent the day taking the letter around Colonia Puesta del Sol. Her greatest success was at the trailer park, whose owner said he received nearly daily complaints from customers, most of them gringos, about barking dogs. He even offered her poison, which she declined. Her greatest defeat came from the acupuncturist, who, despite the loss of his previous dog, replied that only the weak complain about barking.

"I train my dog at four in the morning," he stated, "and when he gets excited, he barks."

"You have no business making a racket at four in the morning," said Maria Eugenia.

"That's when reasonable people get up," he said.

"Fine," she snapped, "and I'm going to train my lion in front of your clinic."

Next she tried one of the walled-in houses, which turned out to belong to no less than the secretary of tourism, a significant figure in the La Paz power structure. The secretary's wife was furious at the barking and eagerly signed the letter. When Maria Eugenia reported her encounter with the acupuncturist, the woman laughed. "I know all about it. He used to train his dog in front of our house before dawn. Our dog is meaner than his, and one morning we let him out. The acupuncturist hasn't been back."

The woman in the adjacent walled-in home was also sympathetic, and by the end of the day, Maria Eugenia felt she had some neighborhood supporters. She had saved the convent for last and ran out of time. While she was away, the fumigator had sprayed the trailer and left a note saying that the invaders were pure honeybees, with no African strain. "Come in and see this," said Maria Eugenia. The trailer's backseat, strewn with shriveled bees, looked like a rack of drying raisins.

After Maria Eugenia left for the convent the next morning, there was a knock on my door. I opened it to confront two nuns. Their red-and-white robes, the black hair in front of their black wimples, their radiant, tea-colored faces were purely dazzling. Were they responding to our noise complaint already? "We're worried about the bees," said one. "We knocked on the trailer yesterday, several times, but nobody answered, and nobody is there now. Did the fumigator come? Did more bees show up? How many bees were there?"

Telling them that the owner of the trailer was, ironically, at the convent right now, I gave what information I had, feeling that two rare quetzals had come to my door. When we finished discussing bees, I said, "By the way, we've been somewhat bothered by the barking dogs on your roof. Would you be willing to take them in at night?"

"We'll be happy to pass that on to the Mother Superior," said the nun who spoke.

As they prepared to leave, I blurted, "Incidentally, I'm a writer and I'm writing about Baja California. Would it be possible to visit the convent sometime?"

"Just ring the doorbell," said the nun, smiling, "and the Mother Superior will be glad to talk to you."

•   •   •

I WAS STARTLED that after Maria Eugenia's mild letter, nocturnal dogs disappeared from the convent roof. I decided to let time pass, to see if the quiet could be trusted, before I rang the convent bell. There was, in any case, much else going on in the Colonia Puesta del Sol. This was an area where La Paz was attempting to cope with its exploding population. In the open field by the kiln, housing for union members was going up in tall, cramped buildings, the owl had decamped, and an American woman I once got a ride to town with remarked, "My, my, La Paz is building the South Bronx." When it rained, the water on the road by the new housing was too deep even for my jeep—though I suspected it had been swelled by a ruptured water main—and the other route involved fording a lagoon by the housing for phosphate miners. Once in a while, city trucks dumped loose sand into the sinkholes, but with nothing to solidify the grains, the sand first impeded traction, then spun out to heighten the ridges, thereby deepening the valleys. Even the secretary of tourism had rough going to his house.

More immediately, the blacksmith had started building a wall of cinder block between his yard and Maria Eugenia's and had gotten as far as her trailer, quitting just short of the A-frame. On the other side, in a vacant lot that included the gutted bus and some large tamarisk trees by the road, a truckful of young men showed up one morning and started another cinder-block wall. In three days they extended it from the street to the A-frame, where they also quit, leaving my view intact and Maria Eugenia's trailer boxed in.

"Who owns the new wall?" I asked Maria Eugenia.

"I don't know," she said. "That's the difference between here and the States. There are no regulations, no limits on what you can do. If your neighbor is absentee, you don't even know who it is unless you plow through the archives at city hall."

"But what's the point of building a wall and stopping?" I asked.

"Another difference. Americans wait until they can finance the whole thing, then they do it all at once. Mexicans start when they have enough money to start, and if they don't get more money, or they get interested in something else, the unfinished thing just sits there, or crumbles."

At last the owner of the vacant lot showed up, saying something vague about raising a small apartment building in back, near the gutted bus. "I don't understand why everybody is putting up these walls," said Maria Eugenia. "They give me claustrophobia."

"I'm just a dentist, lady, not a psychiatrist," he shot back, making her laugh in spite of herself.

I, too, was prey to claustrophobia, and even though I usually left the property during the day, around sunset I grabbed my binoculars and headed on foot toward the bay, either through the South Bronx or past the secretary of tourism's house. Once across the highway I entered the neighborhood where I had lived twenty years before. This was the no-man's-land where I had accompanied a woodgatherer who had hacked at the base of mesquites so that they died on their feet, thereby "cleaning the desert." Now there was no undergrowth left at all. Only the largest trees remained, their extremities shorn, their trunks and crowns still managing a froth of green. Late afternoon, men in pickup trucks pulled up to these amputees with ice chests of Tecate, a beer like fermented dust, and knocked back a few cold ones the way Americans stop at a bar after work. Even though the animated talk over boom-boxed belting ranchera music no doubt obliterated much sense of where they were, there was something wistful about the way the men clung to what little vegetation had been spared.

Through the mesquite parties I threaded my way, listening for anything I could pick up over the speakers. What sailed through clearest was the profanity, along with the odd phrase about jobs or prices or sports, but once, when I lingered by some men with boots and high-crowned hats and guts over their jeans, the talk was of wholesale contracts, markups and legal fees, and I realized that these were entrepreneurs, not the manual laborers I imagined. Halfway through this limbo the dismembered trees gave way to a baseball diamond outlined in old tires, where men often brought their young and teenage sons. Near home plate was a flat rock where a father and son smashed aluminum cans with a smaller rock. Overcoming my inhibitions about bringing trash to what was left of the desert, anonymously and in the morning I left bags of my own empties by the flat rock.

The goal of these walks—to see shorebirds—was anticlimactic on this coast where schools, expensive homes and a biological institute alternated with strips of beach, thick mangroves and pickups of adolescents whose rites also necessitated cranked-up speakers, but typically I would see one blue heron, two night herons, one egret, one snowy egret, pelicans, kingfishers and a pair of Caspian terns. Wandering back to the highway, I tried to retain perspective. Ultimately, this desert was being further cleaned for urban infill; better the improvised park of today than the cramped housing of tomorrow.

Accustomed by now to the convent, tormented less by its dogs, I wrote in the A-frame crow's nest, seldom looking out unless motion caught my eye. I did note more Saturday-morning goat slaughters and saw, with a pang, that the hide of the goat that was half sheep, half fawn was tossed unceremoniously into the wheelbarrow with the rest. And one Saturday afternoon I saw a very different object suspended from the beam: the engine of the little red coupe, raised by block and tackle and being worked on by a pair of mechanics. They were drinking, the glasses revealed, not fermented dust but the same brand of beer that I was. The sight was inviting, and the following day I rounded the domain to the front door, rang the bell and explained I would like to accept an offer to interview the Mother Superior. A fortyish sister said that I was welcome to return the next day at noon. When I left for my appointment, notebook in hand, Maria Eugenia called from the trailer, "Have fun interviewing the deaf one."

THE DOORBELL was answered by the same woman, who introduced herself as Sister Cilia. She invited me to sit down and told me that she, not the Mother Superior, would answer questions. Without waiting for one, she plunged in. "We all have our duties. We sell honey to people who come to the door. We take weather statistics every morning at seven and phone them to a government agency. We make habits for other orders as well as our own, make wedding dresses to specification and dresses for *quinceañeras*—coming-of-age celebrations for girls who turn fifteen. We have a bakery and make cookies, the one thing we distribute ourselves. We also bake the hosts for all the churches of Baja California Sur. And my job is to tend the door. Some days I talk all day, other days I just sit here in silence." This small antechamber, with its white walls, its well-upholstered, anonymous armchairs and table with a few magazines, suggested the waiting room of an expensive, unconsulted doctor.

"Isn't tending the animals another duty?" I asked.

"We do have a string of goats, so we don't buy our meat, but they are tended by a man who is our only paid employee."

"And you also sell goat meat?"

"No." She smiled. "Just the things I mentioned."

Skipping my planned question about the pigs, I asked her to describe a typical day.

"The first bell is at five," she said, mentioning a silvery ring—a discreet sound with which one might summon a maid—that woke me if I was sleeping lightly. "I know the rhythm," I said. "It goes ding-duh-ding, ding-duh-ding."

"Each sister has her own rhythm." She smiled. "There is another bell twenty minutes later"—one that often got me when the first one didn't—"calling us to the first service. Then we have breakfast while one of the sisters reads prayers. Then mass, then each of us goes to her duties. During lunch someone reads religious literature, commentary or the life of a saint, and that person doesn't eat. There are various silences throughout the day, different silences, with different meanings at different hours. We have an hour off in the afternoon, when we can nap or do what we like, and another hour of recreation when we can play games."

"What kind of games?"

"Table games," she said, and I couldn't get her to be more specific. "At dinner there is no religious reading and we can chat casually. Then there is another *servicio divino*, a divine service, in the chapel." Every time she used that expression, which was often, for a split second I heard *servicio de vino*, or wine service.

"We go to bed at nine, but we can stay up later to work on personal projects if we like. We're supposed to be quiet, but sometimes we make noise by mistake," she giggled, while I wondered how anyone would notice over the barking.

"I haven't been aware of the Adorers in the United States," I said. "What is the origin of the order?"

Sister Cilia explained that there were few Adorer convents in the States, so it wasn't surprising I hadn't heard of it. There were a few others, in Canada, Chile, Spain and the founding country of Italy, but the country they flourished in was Mexico, with a thousand nuns in fifty convents. The Perpetual Adorers of the Sacred Sacrament was founded in Rome, in 1807. Maria Magdalena of the Incarnation, a novitiate sweeping the kitchen of another order, had a vision through the wall and into the chapel, where the Virgin, surrounded by flying angels, instructed her to found a special new order dedicated to perpetual prayer. Prayer should be sustained around the clock, with sisters taking turns and prayer itself never stopping. Nuns pray for an hour at a time, and eighteen nuns are considered the minimum feasible number to sustain unceasing prayer. The La Paz convent was built for the classic eighteen but currently numbered only twelve, and they had secured a dispensation from Rome relieving them from praying at night. Nuns in La Paz prayed from dawn to dusk, skipping whatever activity—including meals—they would otherwise be doing at the time.

Convents of Adorers were dying in Italy and blossoming in Mexico, Sister Cilia thought, because Mexican convents were more open, less penitential. "There are convents in Italy built for seventy nuns, with only six old ones left. The sisters in Italy communicate only through iron grilles and never show young people what their life is like, so it isn't surprising they have no recruits. The Italians sent a sister to Mexico to find out how we managed to sustain and increase the order. She saw that it was the openness—that young women, for instance, are allowed to stay with us for a couple of weeks with no obligations, just to see what it is like, to learn that it isn't a prison. The Italian sister went back and reported that to the sisters in Italy, but they didn't want to change. Now there is a program to send Mexican sisters to Italy on five-year stints, to populate the huge empty buildings. The Mexican sisters dread it because it's so sad, so lonely. But just in Baja California we have two new convents opening in Tijuana, another in Mexicali, and our first male branch, a monastery, is also opening in Tijuana."

I had to satisfy my curiosity about a few details, beginning with the blue shell behind their public altar. "A nun who was visiting as the chapel was being built, and who thought it should have something of La Paz, suggested it to the architect. The bronze globe in front was actually my idea. It was made in a local foundry and represents the pearl of the world"—an identification I had missed, possibly because the pearl was set in a scallop shell. And the symbolism of the colorful habits? "White for purity, red for love, black for mortification."

After an hour of conversation I asked if I might see more of the convent itself. Sister Cilia would have to ask the Mother Superior. She returned in five minutes and led me into the courtyard. We were immediately joined by one of the indoor spaniels, who yapped so shrilly I heard nothing else. "Excuse me," said Sister Cilia, "if I don't put her inside, we won't be able to speak."

"Sorry for the mess," she said. "We're going to put tile where the plants are to conserve water. And the roof over that part is falling in. Fortunately, some German millionaires, good people, are giving us the money to fix it." Nuns came and went at the periphery, paying no attention, and at the end of the courtyard I saw the kennel. The three outdoor dogs were confined to a small pen. Stairs on either side of their shaded sleeping area led to the roof, the mysterious shelf I had glimpsed through the foliage. I understood how the dogs, with their elevation and their three-walled sounding board, projected their sound straight to the A-frame, and how the only activity left to them was barking. "Why the kennel?" I asked.

"The dogs protect the fourth side of the courtyard," said Sister Cilia, "and from there they can oversee the whole property. They're our guardians." Dogs, I could see, also had vocations: indoors for affection, outside for protection. On the way out, Sister Cilia gave me three issues of a magazine the convent published and said, "I hope we are being good neighbors to you."

Storing the phrase for possible future use, I returned, somewhat sappily, "And I hope, too, to be a good neighbor," hoping, especially, that the A-frame glass was sufficiently tinted to mask my spying.

RETURNING TO THE YARD, I gave Maria Eugenia a capsule version of the interview. "So they have various businesses going, ask for public alms, take money from Germans, then get a dispensation from the Pope because twelve nuns can't keep up round-the-clock prayer."

"I don't think they're selling goat in the market," I said, but by then the screen door to the trailer had snapped shut, with Maria Eugenia behind it.

As for me, I enjoyed knowing what the silvery ball meant, how the tricolored species spent its time, how the dogs blasted through the foliage. If the secrets, disclosed, were banal, I could still better imagine their life. As spring advanced, volleyball games materialized on Sunday afternoons, with the younger nuns in their blue work uniforms teamed with assorted young men. Whether the latter were family members, parishioners or pickup players from the neighborhood, I'm sure the Italian Adorers would have been scandalized. I, in turn, was scandalized when a hole was breached in the wall by the goat pen, Bass Lake hacked down some old mesquites inside the wall, and the goats disappeared. Suddenly the area filled with spools of phone cable, moved from the storage yard across the street. Did the phone company offer so much for storage that the nuns now bought their meat with the rent money? Were they turning vegetarian? The unplanted field behind the A-frame seemed doubly empty without the mock battles, the sarcastic bleats, the butting and leaping. I read the three magazines Sister Cilia had given me and found them to be full of articles about peninsular history and culture, with less religious propaganda than I expected. I also noted that an article soliciting donations for the new roof included the unlisted convent phone number.

One night, after a period of relative calm, one of the indoor spaniels—surely the one Sister Cilia put inside so we could talk—began to shriek like one of those soprano trumpets used for baroque music. After two hours I got up and dialed the number in the magazine. On the twelfth ring I gave up. When the dog screeched again the following night, I marched to the convent the next morning, prepared to tell Sister Cilia it was time to deliver on the good-neighbor policy. With so many special silences, how about one for sleeping? A different nun answered the door; perhaps it was Sister Cilia's hour to pray. When I explained the problem, the new nun said, "That dog protects us."

"The dog is too small to protect anyone," I objected. "It just barks for the sake of barking."

She gazed at me with a sweet, impenetrable smile as I went on. "We're your neighbors, and we were sleepless for hours." I stopped for her to reply, but she was as fixed as the Mona Lisa. "If a dog barks nonstop," I said, "how can you tell when it's finally barking *at* something? It all sounds the same."

The nun maintained her sweet, stonewalling smile and

finally said, "I'll tell the Mother Superior about it." When I left, I decided that the Mother Superior was the circular file.

The spaniel did stop, but three nights later the outdoor dogs were back. I dialed the convent with no expectations, but a sister answered. "Your dogs are barking," I said wearily, "and your neighbors can't sleep. Would you mind taking them in?"

"We can't. They're on the roof."

"I *know* they're on the roof. Please take them *off* the roof."

"But they bother us, too!" she said, with a commiseration so surreal that I hung up. But the sisters achieved a miracle, for the barking ceased.

I had taken over from Maria Eugenia in trying to muzzle the night and kept her abreast. "It's ironic," she said, "that those with the most faith feel the most insecure, the most in need of protection. Also the most professionally selfless are the most willing to bother their neighbors. But you must recognize two things. One, they take orders from the Mother Superior, who wouldn't hear a wolfhound bellowing on her pillow. The other is that noise *is* the sound of security for them, because it's their noise. The dogs don't have to be barking at anything. As long as they're barking, defensive noise, harm can't reach them."

Suddenly I saw it. Aimless barking informed the world you were feeding a set of fangs. Danger at night came stealthily, silently, and if you were vulnerable on one side, you raised a wall of sound. Steady, random firing into the night, barking— or an alarm system, or a boom box—was a lullaby you sang to yourself. It was noisy in La Paz, in the rest of Mexico, in the rest of Latin America, in most of the world where isolation wasn't its own defense. Earlier I had hoped to be repaid for my insomnia with a diverting scandal about poison and pigs, but instead I left the A-frame possessed of an Orwellian revelation. Noise is peace.

DURING THE EARLY NINETIES I became aware that a new word was circulating in La Paz, borrowed from the English. The word was *privacy* and so fresh was the loan that speakers weren't sure how it went. Was it *privacía* or *privacidad*? There had always been the adjective *privado*, as in *propriedad privada* for private property and *hablar en privado* for talking in private. There was even *la vida privada* for private life. But unlike other Anglicisms for which there was a perfectly good equivalent in Spanish, like *troke* instead of *camión* for truck, or *raite* instead of *aventón* for ride, the word *privacy* was borrowed, I felt, because it filled an actual need. The closest equivalent was *intimidad*, but intimacy didn't include such aspects as, say, confidentiality. The reason for the conscription, I decided, was that the concept of privacy in all its English-speaking ramifications was only now reaching critical mass in a city like

Infectious
Laughter

La Paz because so many of its inhabitants had spent time in the privacy-oriented States.

I had experienced no variations in privacy between La Paz and the United States, living solo as I did in a rental apartment and socializing with whom I pleased at home and abroad, and the differences surfaced only during what I would call adventures in medicine. These appeared gradually, for most of the time in La Paz I was in excellent health. I drank tap water without ill effects until local friends prevailed upon me to switch to the purified, and the only time I got sick on the food was at an American-owned restaurant. When I did go to the doctor for a knee problem, a skin rash, the only difference was that instead of making an appointment and waiting with the problem, often I could see the doctor immediately or later the same day. I had, as backup, an offer from a winemaker who lived two blocks from me and once said, as a neighborly gesture, that if I ever needed quick medical help, he had an in with the military hospital, which was also in the neighborhood and had a reputation for being much better than La Paz's general hospital, the Salvatierra.

Several years after that offer I woke up with a stinging pain in my left arm, from shoulder to wrist. The skin was red and spiky, and I theorized that on a desert ramble I had collided with some noxious plant. I walked swiftly to the winemaker, who heard my description, saw my arm and continued the walk to the hospital. He informed the receptionist who he was and who he knew, and after a brief exchange on the intercom the hospital's head doctor came down the stairs. The doctor apologized that the specialist in such cases was on vacation but he would handle it himself. We followed him to his office on the top floor.

I bared my arm, describing the pain and its probable cause.

The doctor held my arm to the light. "The redness is following your arterial system. This has nothing to do with a plant. Did you ever have chicken pox as a child?"

"Yes."

"It can recur in another form during adulthood. You have *Varicela zoster.*" Mention of chicken pox informed me that I had just heard the Latin for what Americans call shingles. "I'll write you a prescription for a painkiller, which you can pick up at a pharmacy across the street." When I pulled out my wallet to pay for the visit, the doctor delivered a crisp "No charge." After a three-block march back home, I marveled that I had been diagnosed and issued an analgesic within a half hour, a feat surely impossible in the United States. It hadn't occurred to me that there was anything unusual in the winemaker, a third party, being present during my consultation with the doctor, since it was he who had brought this miracle about.

But the painkiller didn't work. In acute distress, I continued normal socializing as a distraction, and it was a relief to unload my tribulation on friends. Our circle of amateur pianists met in the quarters of a veterinarian who lived with her spinet above her clinic. "Let me check the medicine," said Alejandrina after hearing my story. She pulled out a dictionary-sized tome, paged it, peered into minuscule print, then announced, "He prescribed the wrong medicine. I'll write you a prescription for the right one." She fetched a small pad, scribbled, then handed me the slip. Above her writing was printed *Clínica Veterinaria Cuatro Molinos.*

"When I show it to the pharmacist," I asked, "should I bark?"

The next morning I took the prescription to the main pharmacy on the plaza, fully expecting to be asked whether it was my dog or cat who had the shingles, but the pharmacist filled it without comment and it worked. The episode occurred shortly before my return north, so I drove home as best I could, turned the case over to my home doctor and billed my American insurance.

It was a full decade before my next encounter with La Paz medicine, this time in the winemaker's role of impresario. For years my rancher friend Lico had suffered breathing difficulties because of a deviated septum, a minor problem on the ranch that turned acute on necessary visits to the agricultural town of Constitución, which was bulldozing its streets ever farther into the desert. As they waited for pavement, the streets blew dust through town—dust that might be implicated in Lico's endless flus and colds, none of which I ever caught. Because he needed to return to Constitución often for supplies, and family members needed a place to stay when they required medical attention, he kept a small house there. For years the town's doctors had pressed upon him the need for a septum operation, but along with dreading the knife, Lico distrusted the quality of medicine in Constitución. More recently, meanwhile, in an effort to trim his swelling paunch, he had relatives hold his knees flat to the ground while he performed sit-ups, stressing his lumbar so as to throw out his back and trigger sciatica. He found no reliable help for that either in Constitución, and these agonies needed relief before we could realize our plans to explore and camp in obscure corners of the surrounding mountains. I told him I would canvas friends in La Paz and line up the appropriate specialists.

When I inquired about deviated septum authorities, I learned that the best ear, nose and throat doctor was a man I already knew socially, an eccentric with a keen interest in contemporary classical music. A chiropractor had been recommended to me by an environmentalist whose back he had relieved when no one else could, an experience that resonated with me because the right chiropractor had untied a knot of my own that had defied all other practitioners, from orthopedists to therapists to other chiropractors. I swung by his clinic, to be greeted by a sandwich board that listed services, proceeding through adjustment, massage and reflexology to aromatherapy. This latter fell into a category I called assholistic medicine but I continued through the door, to be greeted by a woman who described herself as the doctor's professional partner. The doctor was always in, she said, though he wasn't at the moment, and one could make an appointment on the day one wanted it. I had done my homework for Lico's visit, which didn't occur until a month later, when he was over his latest flu.

HE ARRIVED on a Sunday night, we had garrulous beers in my apartment, and Lico wondered if the chiropractor would attack his malt-swollen stomach. When I suggested, in rancher mode, that his best move was a late-term abortion, he texted the option to his overweight La Paz nephew. The next morning I drove Lico to his appointments, beginning with the chiropractor.

The doctor was out but the woman made an appointment for later in the afternoon, then snapped, "So what's your problem besides bad posture?" Lico explained it and the woman offered him free reflexology. I explained that reflexology was massage that relaxed the foot muscles, releasing tension and radiating stability upward. As Lico pulled off his high-heeled, pointed ochre boots with a grid of bumps on the surface, the woman glared, then snapped, "What is that, snake?"

"Ostrich," replied Lico.

"Poor ostriches," she sighed. "There aren't many left."

"There's a whole ranch of them outside Constitución," he shot back.

For the rest of the visit, whenever Lico wrestled his boots on or off we riffed on the exchange. "Poor chipmunks," I would sigh. "Poor whales. Poor rats. There aren't many left."

On to the septum specialist. It was a pleasure to see my friend Maurilio again after a several-year absence, and after our warm greetings I tried to find the waiting room, but there was only a person-wide standing space by the front door. I retreated there, prepared for a long stand, when Maurilio peered at me, baffled, and boomed, "Come in and sit down!" Mozart played in the background and I had a ringside view as Maurilio shone a laserlike flashlight up Lico's nose. We discussed the possibility that Lico's incessant colds and flus might be unvented allergies, and he pronounced that Lico didn't need an operation for what could be handled with drugstore nasal sprays. Lico looked immensely relieved as Maurilio handed him a spray. As Lico skimmed a list of what not to eat or drink to make sure beer hadn't made the cut, the doctor turned to me and asked, "Do you know Górecki's Third Symphony?"

"I do indeed," I replied. "The definitive recording was conducted by David Zinman, director of the Aspen Music Festival in my hometown. It won a Grammy for best classical recording of the year."

"I don't remember who conducted my CD," said Maurilio.

"It will be Zinman," I assured him.

"Do you know the music of Arvo Pärt?" he asked, naming a contemporary Estonian composer.

"I've heard a bit but know more from reading about him."

"You need to listen, not read," instructed Maurilio.

Lico looked at us with the same blankness I register when he and his friends discuss horse racing in Constitución.

A bite to eat, then on to the chiropractor.

At last the doctor was in, loud and loquacious, and he, too, invited me to accompany the patient. Lico mentioned the sciatica, the inability to climb or descend. The doctor ordered Lico to strip to his shorts, and said, "I'll make my own investigation." As he did so, he pattered on about country food versus city food, friends on ranches, his favorite towns. Having been to numerous chiropractors, always with preliminary anxiety, I found the manipulations reassuringly standard, if roughly done. I knew that Lico didn't like to be seen in public without his boots, but empowered to intrude, I asked whether Lico's high heels, elevating his bottom, didn't create an aggravating curve in his lumbar. Heels tightened the Achilles tendon, shortened the calf muscles . . . The chiropractor replied that the boots didn't help, but Lico was used to them. He then asked me to steady Lico's shoulder while he performed a leg maneuver, first one side, then the other. I marveled at my hands-on role in the day's medicine, since I had been to countless chiropractors and none had required a helper, let alone an untrained onlooker. Lico would need three sessions, with a day of rest between them, which meant we were to return Wednesday and Friday. Meanwhile, something had to be done about Lico's paunch, because all that weight in front was throwing his back out.

"I've tried exercise and dieting," said Lico, "but it doesn't seem to work."

"That's because your intestines are blocked. You need a purgative before the diet. I'm going to give you something for that. It's rather like a nut. You cut it in half and eat half. You will have mild diarrhea and perhaps experience nausea, but it won't be severe. Before you take it, you should drink some *suero*." The word meant "serum," but was commonly used for a syrupy energy drink.

"That's all?" asked Lico. I listened closely and asked him to repeat the instructions, since I would have to field whatever consequences.

"Yes, just cut it in half and eat half." He disappeared, then returned with what looked like a large mahogany button. Lico dressed and slipped it into his breast pocket. We agreed to meet the same time Wednesday.

As we drove home, I marveled to Lico that I, the mere driver, was a participant in the consultation. Lico was surprised at my surprise. "The doctor always includes whoever you're with."

"What if there are details you don't want the person you're with to know about? What," I pressed, "if you injured yourself with a stupid fall when you were drunk? What if you had a sexually transmitted disease? What if you didn't want your problem to become gossip?"

"I suppose you would try to go to the doctor alone."

"And if you couldn't get there alone?"

"Then you would just have to decide. Not tell the whole story to the doctor, or tell it and ask who you're with not to spread it."

"It sounds to me like a breach of *privacidad*," I said, using the version that had prevailed. Lico didn't reply, either because the word and its concept hadn't made it to Constitución or else to end a tedious exchange.

When we reached my apartment, Lico's nephew dropped by for a visit and Lico regaled him with his medical adventures. The overweight nephew asked if he could have the other half of the purgative so he could start his own diet. Lico pulled the little rondure out of his shirt pocket and cut it in half, giving his nephew the slightly smaller portion. When the nephew left, full of thanks, Lico placed his own half-nut on my kitchen counter. As he chugged the *suero*, I scanned the exposed cross-section of what appeared to be fine but inedible layers of wood. Lico popped it in and began to chew.

While I didn't clock it, the chewing seemed to last a half hour before Lico downed the last bits. He lay down to wait for something to happen. Nothing did for two hours. In his stomach there was a sudden stab of pain. He got up clutching his paunch and settled on the sofa. We sat for more than an hour mainly in silence, although Lico occasionally mumbled, "This is awful." Now and then he headed to the bathroom for what he described as a small watery movement. I sat helpless. Lico sat up with a lurch and gasped, "Quick, fan me! I can't breathe!" I grabbed a notebook and began fanning furiously. He did breathe, but in convulsions. "Get me an onion!" he cried.

"I don't *have* an onion."

"Go buy one!"

No stores were open at eleven p.m., nor would I have gone shopping with a friend dying on the sofa. I suddenly remembered my landlady downstairs and dialed with one hand while I fanned with the other. She answered on the fourth ring.

"Have you an onion?"

"Just one."

I dashed downstairs, raced up with the onion, cut it in half and held it to his nose while grabbing the notebook with my other hand and fanning from the side. Fumes or placebo, Lico gradually managed increasing gasps of oxygen and some twenty minutes later was back to breathing normally. After a stupor of recovery, physical on his part and emotional on mine, he said he wanted to go back to bed. He got up unsteadily, as if drunk; I grabbed his elbow and we steered cautiously toward the bed. I pulled up a cot mattress on the floor near him and rested my head on a pillow, ready to field whatever came next.

Lico turned and shifted once in a while, and sometimes lightly snored, while I waited and dozed off. Suddenly he was speaking. "I need some *suero*. Right now."

"Where?" I asked, glancing at the clock. "It's quarter to five."

"Any Oxxo," he said, naming a convenience store. "They're open around the clock."

The emptiness of the streets was eerie. In fifteen minutes I was back with *suero* and an assortment of fruit juices. Lico chugged a bottle of *suero* straight, followed by a chaser of apple juice. He returned to bed and fell rehydrated into a snoring coma.

At eight a.m., with daylight pouring like a lifeline through the windows, we were both up and talking. The stomach pains had subsided to a low ache and breath was normal. Over my coffee and Lico's manzanilla tea, the postmortems began. "When you were fanning me," said Lico, "I saw multiple images of you dancing around me. And when I sent you for the *suero*, I was immediately terrified. I was sure you would be abducted and I had sent you to your death. When you came back through the door was the happiest moment of my life."

I was deeply moved by Lico's anxiety but answered, "The only thing on the street was a squad car driving at a crawl with its lights flashing. It made me nervous but they left me alone. What's the business with the onion?"

"When they were rebuilding the primary school at San José," he said, naming the town, population forty, a kilometer from his ranch, "they hired a construction crew from Constitución. One of the workers brought his wife and a child who was epileptic. Whenever the child was about to have a seizure, they cut an onion and held it to his nose, which fended off the attack. When someone in Agua Verde was about to have an epileptic seizure, I tried it myself. I cut an onion and held it up to him and the attack didn't happen." He didn't draw the connection between these cases and himself, since his problem wasn't epilepsy, but he probably saw the onion as a system-changer in a crisis. Cause or coincidence, after its fumes he did begin to recover his breath. He called his nephew, whose agony included a small protrusion of intestine through his anus. Horrified, he pushed it back in, where it remained. He thought, *If I'm this near death, my uncle, who is twenty years older, must be dead.*

We had nothing scheduled that day except another chiropractic appointment at four p.m., and spent most of the time catching up on sleep. I received a call from a Puerto Rican friend who wanted to schedule lunch. When I described the night's events, he said it reminded him of a medieval remedy called *nux vomica*, Latin for "vomit nut," based on the homeopathic notion that a dab of poison rallies the body against larger doses.

We returned to the chiropractor and Lico unloaded the story. The doctor expressed shock. That would be a one-in-a-thousand reaction. He had been giving the purgative out free for years and nobody had experienced such a thing. "Here," he said, pulling open a drawer full of brown buttons, "look at all these. Nothing happens." I wasn't sure what the quantity of buttons was supposed to prove, but the nephew's experience made Lico's convulsions seem not so rare. Lico repeated his story, adding that the thing was so tough it took nearly a half hour to chew.

"You didn't eat the husk too?" asked the chiropractor.

"*Husk?*" repeated Lico. "You didn't say anything about a husk."

"You were supposed to pull out the seed and just eat that." The tone was didactic, teacher to child.

"Your instructions were to cut it in half and eat half. And drink *suero*. And that's *all*." Lico glared.

"We had you repeat the instructions," I added, "and I listened closely because I would be tending my friend."

Lico and I took turns repeating what he had said until the chiropractor, abashed, admitted that he must have forgotten that part. I wondered how he could have omitted key information when asked to repeat, but we proceeded straight to the treatment. The chiropractor made a bit of small talk but gone was Monday's banter. Again I was asked to hold Lico's shoulders for the leg maneuver. As we were paying and preparing to leave, with one treatment to go, I asked the name of the purgative.

"*Haba de San Ignacio.*"

When we were back in the apartment, I asked Lico if his back was any better.

"Possibly. It's hard to tell."

"I've been to a number of chiropractors and his maneuvers look quite standard. If you don't ingest anything else, he might actually do you some good."

Lico didn't answer. In the morning he said that the Friday treatment was the only appointment still pending in La Paz and he didn't feel like waiting another day for it. It was a relief that he felt no aftereffect from the evil nut, but one near-death experience was enough of La Paz for one visit. I didn't try to detain him.

As soon as he had driven off, I googled *haba de San Ignacio*. I read some ten sites in Spanish, and when I encountered one with a list of the phenomena in various languages, I visited more sites for "Saint Ignatius bean" in English. Conditions it was taken for included epilepsy, depression, sexual dysfunction, inability to express negative moods, hysteria and insomnia, with mental problems outnumbering the physical. The shrub was native to the Philippines and was encountered by Captain Cook and other European explorers. On learning that indigenous people used it as a multipurpose remedy, colonials distributed it throughout the temperate world. One site said that it was similar in effect to nux vomica, though milder. In Mexico it was grown primarily in the state of Coahuila. The stunner was that the principal ingredient was "estricnina." I save the italics for the English: *strychnine*. The sites themselves were positive, neutral and negative. One in Spanish called it "a violent purgative . . . causing severe neurological deterioration, loss of consciousness, psychomotor agitation and crisis convulsions." A site in English concluded USAGE HIGHLY DANGEROUS.

IT WAS IN MY CONTACT with medicine, scant as it was, that I found a corner of La Paz culture in which north-of-the-border privacy was replaced by other virtues. A physician's prescription had been corrected by a veterinarian, I had helped with a chiropractic move that had always been performed on me by the practitioner alone, I'd been dispensed advice on Estonian music, and I had a chance to give the patient a second opinion about the doctors—touches both amusing and useful. Operating theaters for doctors had their analog in consultational theaters for the patient's companions, and the sessions I attended were largely comic. Even the husk of the St. Ignatius bean turned to wisecrack once the trauma receded. Medicine survived became entertainment from an unlikely quarter.

But strychnine can kill, and disease is funny only if you can look back, recovered, with someone who shared the script. Illness, physical or otherwise, is the great calamity that can end in life's opposite. Faced with symptoms, I will consult without sidekick. I will share only details of my choosing. I will down my meds in privacy, leaving the word untranslated.

TOO MUCH HAS BEEN MADE of desert sunsets, particularly in the captions of oversaturated magazine photos. Because desert skies tend to be clear, they can't match the Midwest for cloud effects or smog-inflamed cities for sheer longevity. But they are inferior only to novices who look, naively, in the direction of the setting sun, for the real desert sunset occurs in that unlikely direction, the east. It is opposite the sun that the last rays, deflected through clear skies, fall on the long, minutely eroded mountain ranges and bathe our eyes with light of decreasing wavelengths and cooling colors—vermilion to salmon to plum—transporting the eastern horizon to islands of pure yearning.

The desert rat, so in love with distance that he commonly carries binoculars to bring it up close, instinctively focuses the dreamlike mountains to heighten the effect. Here an odd

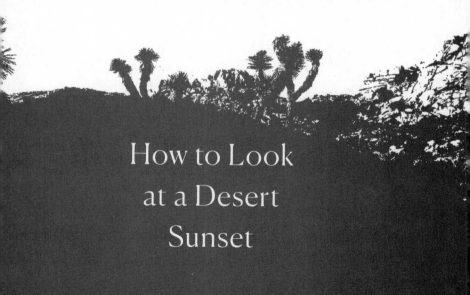

How to Look at a Desert Sunset

reversal takes place, for what is plum to the naked eye, confined and enlarged, turns drab as cement, while the heaped knobs and extravagant spires turn out to be exfoliated granite. The observer knows how this stone weathers into rounded piles, how it crumbles underfoot, how it is colonized by black lichen. Fascinating as geology, it has been mastered by experience, turned to stone.

That is the revelation of desert sunsets: that the distance is so unmoored, so delicious, that you want to be there, to *become* that distance. And the closer you come—quickly, through binoculars, because it darkens even as you watch—the faster it burns into the ash of reality. Then you find out that where you want to be is precisely where you began, stripped to your bare eyes, watching as best you can, yearning.

LA PAZ, WHICH HAD PRODUCED nothing of global significance since the pearl beds dried up in the late 1930s, slowly became aware through rumor and news stories that it was targeted for what was being billed as "the eclipse of the century," a blackening of the sun that might draw up to a million people, four times the city's own population. Furthermore, some of those people might be, in the root sense, lunatics.

There was no denying the astronomical significance. Although the sun's diameter is four hundred times that of the moon, the moon is four hundred times closer to the earth, so one can cover the other like coins of the same denomination. Of the several dozen moons in our solar system, no other creates on a planetary surface that perfect fit, blotting the sun while revealing its entire corona. Yet within that congruence lies a bit of play. The duration of an eclipse is extended when

Black Pearl

the earth is farthest from the sun, rendering the sun small, and when the moon is nearest the earth, rendering the moon large. The July 11, 1991, eclipse approached the maximum of a far sun and a close moon, and its duration in Baja California Sur—six minutes and twenty-one seconds—would be one minute and one second short of the longest eclipse possible. Solar eclipses occur on earth on an average of every eighteen months, but most are brief, or visible only at sea, or at uncomfortable polar latitudes, or in countries at war. In North America the most recent lengthy solar eclipse was in 1806, with the next to occur in 2132.

The astronomical community hasn't been surprised by eclipses for hundreds of years and had been planning for this one at least a decade in advance. Its path would begin just after dawn on the Big Island of Hawaii, cross the Pacific to arrive in Baja California Sur near noon, then continue its arc over mainland Mexico and Central America to expire in Brazil. This would be the first major eclipse to pass over an important observatory, at Mauna Kea in Hawaii, and Mauna Kea seemed, scientifically, the obvious choice. But Mauna Kea was likely to be socked in. Baja California promised the clearest weather in the eclipse's path, and many scientists preferred La Paz. The centerline, or core of the moon's shadow, was to pass seventy miles south of the city, but the most serious calibration, such as measuring the sun's expansion and contraction by the moon's edge, is best done *away* from the centerline, making La Paz the optimum spot.

The University of La Paz, perched on a hill behind town, was slated to become base camp for scientific teams from fifteen countries. With funding from the Mexican government, the university acquired six hundred cots, set up banking and postal services, hired round-the-clock medical attention, and provided telex, photocopiers, fax, cafeterias and hourly bus service to town. The scientific community, more attached to its subculture—or superculture—than to its points of origin on the five continents, was well prepared to converge on La Paz for its six-minute opportunity.

Outside the penumbra of science, eclipses have a reputation for disaster. The word derives from the Greek *ekleipsis*, meaning "abandonment." Eclipses were said to have preceded Assyrian insurrections and the distruction of the Athenian navy. According to Chinese myth from the Bamboo Annals, the sun went into eclipse in 1952 B.C. when the sky tenders got drunk. In Amos 8, Jehovah threatens a disobedient Israel with a solar eclipse, along with sackcloth, lamentations and universal baldness. In Pindar's "Ninth Ode," written after an eclipse in Thebes in 463 B.C., pillage of the daystar threatens the loss of man's strength and wisdom, along with war, heat, frost and a Noah-like flood that might refashion humanity. In A.D. 840, an eclipse caused the emperor of Bavaria to die of fright. One would expect steadier nerves four centuries after Copernicus, but in 1983, in Indonesia, the military chased everyone indoors before occultation, then got chased indoors themselves by their superiors. Closer to La Paz, in a Canadian schoolyard where astronomers had set up their scopes in 1979, the schoolmaster herded all of his students inside to watch TV, then ran outside and yelled at the scientists, "Get in, get in, the eclipse is coming!"

Mexico had its Aztec and Mayan legends involving gods who battle for control of the sky, as well as a heroic Toltec martyr who made an alliance with the Plumed Serpent to rescue the sun. In La Paz eclipse fears took a more contemporary turn. Attendance estimates soared when it was suggested that clans of New Agers, dripping with crystals, would converge for weird ceremonies. It would be the "Woodstock of astronomy." Towns along the way would run out of food, water and gas, or would set up impromptu tollbooths. Most of La Paz's six thousand guest beds had been booked up to two years in advance, and the Mexican government floated the idea of allowing only the first 25,000 cars south of Ensenada, or of requiring proof of hotel reservations. Mary Shroyer, managing the Marina de La Paz, says that a roadblock was proposed at Guerrero Negro, with travelers required to get stickers ahead of time. Many tried almost daily for two months to get stickers but kept being told that they hadn't arrived rather than that the plan had been scrapped. Americans, who like everything lined up in advance, were put off, and some canceled. It was both confirmed and denied that valuable equipment would have to be registered with customs agents. Such mixed signals characterized the official approach. Many Paceños arranged privately to rent their homes to eclipseniks and were supposed to pay the Office of Tourism a fee and open their houses for inspection. The government bought hundreds of tents to arrange in tent cities, to cost sixty dollars a night. The two accessible airports, at La Paz and Los Cabos, could handle only a limited number of planes, and those who flew in would have to stagger their arrivals and departures—spending up to a week in La Paz for their six dark minutes.

The winter before it happened, I sifted rumors and opportunities. My one personal association with solar eclipses was when my father took me to watch a partial solar eclipse on the shores of Lake Michigan when I was seven or eight. I remember how strange it was to watch him hold burning matches under a piece of glass until it was nearly black, then drive five blocks to the lake, hold it to the sky, and make me promise to look *only* through the sooty glass. I remember nothing of what

I saw in the heavens, only the strangeness of my father's concern. Then I read Annie Dillard's terrifying account of a solar eclipse in *Teaching a Stone to Talk*, published in 1982, in which the black wall of the moon's shadow races toward the onlookers at twice the speed of sound, making them scream. I decided then that I would travel anywhere for the experience, and I couldn't believe that a solar eclipse of maximum duration and the peninsula of my obsession were poised for conjunction. I wanted to watch the eclipse alone in the desert, to listen to the birds fall silent and watch the lizards freeze. I wanted to watch the eclipse and to watch Baja California watch the eclipse: wanted Dillard's pure racing shadow and my father's worried hand on the glass.

Baja Expeditions, which had previously sent no more than 300 clients out kayaking, bicycling, scuba diving and whale watching at a time, was planning to disperse 800 people into boats, hotels and a beach camp. Their most curious contingent was a party of 360 Japanese, to be stashed in three La Paz hotels and a convent, who would watch from the convent roof. That option was closed to non-Japanese, but there were also various boats and hotels plus a beach camp for 170 customers south of La Paz, in the centerline, with lecturing astronomers on staff. The edge of the eclipse might be better for experiments, but even off-duty astronomers preferred the deep middle for sheer thrills. So it was to be the Centerline Camp, with time before and afterward in La Paz, to sample its moment in the occulted sun.

WHEN I LANDED in La Paz, a week before the event, the temperature was in the pleasant eighties rather than the predicted hundreds and traffic was little denser than normal. Gift shops bulged with eclipse mugs, ashtrays, paperweights of black rocks painted with orange coronas, and T-shirts with such messages as "I Blacked Out in Baja" and "Darkness at Noon," but the streets sported only a modest number of tourists and not one crystallized New Ager. Baja Expeditions headquarters was another matter, for besides its own 800 clients to be processed, every foreigner with an independent project had heard that Baja Expeditions was a clearinghouse for information, and they haunted its social facilities. Along with the expected media teams, there was a Canadian film crew that was working on an eclipse tale set in Toronto, had planned to fake the special effects, then decided to catch the real thing in Baja California and screen out the cactus. *The New York Times* had sent its science team to Hawaii, and reporters dispatched to La Paz from the regular bureau were hoping Hawaii would be socked in, allowing them to scoop the specialists. One man planned to watch for behavioral changes at a sea lion rookery, and another—in the only twist to eclipse watching I would willingly skip—intended to spend the event underwater, filming fish going to sleep.

Maria Eugenia took a *New York Times* reporter, a writer from *Outside*, and me to the Convent of St. Bridget, where she was directing the food operation for the Japanese. Everything needed to be coordinated to the minute, for they would be jetting to La Paz for twenty-four hours, watching the eclipse on jet lag, then jetting back to Japan. Rather than round-the-clock prayer, this convent's service was to keep a retreat of quiet rooms for rent around a shaded courtyard, with attendance at religious services not required but certainly convenient. The nuns had only been contacted at the last minute, when one of the hotels canceled, and Sister Julia Nazareth, from India, was supervising the installation of fifty extra cots, doubling the capacity of the nuns' hostel. Exuding calm, Sister Julia said she was looking forward to visitors from her own hemisphere. Maria Eugenia took us next to the university, where astronomers from Russia, Japan, Czechoslovakia, Korea, Germany, the United States and elsewhere were setting up instruments. On the hour, guides explained which contingent was doing what. Oblivious of the tours, astronomers strolled between trailers and night scopes, some of them in bikinis that would raise eyebrows on Mexican beaches, and the fact that they could only be observed from behind rope made them seem oddly like primates from space.

Amid these pockets of bustle, La Paz residents remained ambivalent and confused. Congratulated on winning the celestial lottery, they were warned that certain materials marketed to protect their eyes were untrustworthy, then assured that no damage was possible during the full eclipse, or totality. Many were so fearful for their eyes that they planned to watch this event—to which zealots were winding from around the world—on TV. The civic cultural center featured two eclipse-oriented art shows, one depicting the eclipse in mythology, the other displaying local art that showed the sun occluded by cactus fruit, the Aztec sun stone superimposed on the sun, and a solar eclipse presiding over an erupting volcano and a city in flames. Remarked the show's curator with some vehemence, "Advertisers want people to watch their commercial instead of the sky, so they're deliberately scaring them inside to their sets. This, in a country where pre-Columbian astronomy was so sophisticated that observations were lined up not just with the sun and moon, but with the stars."

On my last pre-eclipse evening in La Paz, I was one of forty people who went to the Teatro de la Ciudad to see *El Eclipse*, a drama by the prominent Mexican playwright Carlos Olmos. The show had run successfully for six months in Mexico City before being brought to La Paz for a one-night stand. A young man pretending to be a photographer who had come to shoot the eclipse is the lone guest at a battered seaside resort run by three generations of women and the lone surviving male, aged twenty-five. One assumes that the newcomer will be variously entangled with the women and fended off by the man, but it devolves that the men had previously met in Mexico City and fallen in love. As the world dims, the dramatic buildup touches on drug money, the influence on Mexico of gringos and the Japanese, the impact of mourning on teen clothing, and whether to sell foreigners some family property. During stage blackout a second-generation woman, secretly pregnant, wears red ribbons under her clothing to protect her unborn from strange rays, another woman watches totality through her late husband's X-rays, and local children, offstage, beat drums to help the sun escape from the moon. As light returns the two men take off in the family van, leaving the women without males and without wheels. In a program note, the playwright says he intended to reflect on his characters' intimate contradictions during a night of cosmic terror, and if the experience of actual sky watchers was less turgid, there was no denying that the eclipse was an inspired plot device for throwing characters and themes together.

NOT KNOWING whether La Paz was enjoying the lull before a storm or whether it had spooked a bonanza, I boarded a used school bus that Baja Expeditions had brought for the eclipse and bailed out two hours later at their beach camp. The instant village for more than two hundred, including staff, had

been pitched just north of Rancho Leonero, a small sportfish-
ing hotel on a secluded bluff. For weeks an Expeditions employee had wrestled with the site, hacking a shaded dining
area from a tamarisk thicket, setting up a tank with sixty thousand gallons of water as an emergency supplement to groundwater, raising a resort with cooking, socializing and sleeping
areas under the starry sky. He was away when the bulldozer
he had ordered to smooth the beach and dune top churned them
up instead, and he wound up leveling the area himself by
dragging a car bumper from a pickup, a device he referred to
as a Fresno. By the time we arrived, ninety tents had been
lined up like turquoise barnacles on the dune, with another
thirty in a grove of young palms. Shadowy figures looked busy
through the mosquito netting of the cook tent, then sun was
warming fresh water for gravity-fed showers, a large canvas
roof on the beach offered shade between pipes that released a
pressurized mist, and a parachute silk was luffing in anticipa-
tion of happy hour.

Yesterday's busload had already settled in, and busloads
were to arrive for the next three days until the camp was full
for blackout. While jokes circulated about "high noon for
nerds," it was hard to isolate an eclipse type. Older people in
the professions predominated, many of them amateur astronomers since childhood. Teachers, a city planner, a river guide, a
priest, an off-duty photographer, the assistant attorney general
of Illinois and a woman writing for a hometown weekly introduced themselves over tamales. A computer programmer who
used the distribution of solar eclipses to explore the world said
that during the Indonesian eclipse he wound up touring all day,
napping from seven to eleven, and stargazing all night. A concert pianist claimed to find similarities in the spectra of sound
and light. A retired accountant said he had come "because

watching a partial eclipse is like kissing your sister." A resident of Hawaii, in the path of totality at home, correctly guessed his state would be clouded over, and did a brisk business in Hawaiian T-shirts featuring King Kamehameha brandishing a black sun. A bicoastal family had been planning this as a reunion ever since one member saw a total eclipse in Helena, Montana, in 1979. One woman was escaping the penumbra of the Empire State Building, and another arrived from Minnesota bearing a sack of energy bars and two gallons of water, despite having prepaid for all the amenities, because her local paper had used the dire phrase "Woodstock of astronomy." The camp's champion eclipse chaser was racking up his sixth solar. I felt my greatest affinity with a retired physician who had also been exploring the peninsula since 1968 and had come largely because it was "a big Baja event."

In preparation for the eclipse we gathered under the parachute, or in the shade with the mist machine, to listen to six resident lecturers, including a cosmologist, an infrared astronomer, and an astronaut-in-waiting. "It's best to know all you can ahead," said a U.S. Navy astronomer just back from the Gulf War, "because an eclipse is delicious terror, a roller coaster, and you'll miss too much by being overwhelmed." As he explained the sun's chromosphere, however, it was difficult not to let one's gaze drift from the parachute silk out to the sun's photons pouring on date palms full of orioles, the thorny brush of the dunes, the blues of the Sierra de la Laguna dancing inland. At either end of the dune sat telescopes like an orchestral brass section, with owners who invited passersby to peer at the phenomena visible by day: sunspots, Venus going through phases like the moon. The least morning mist, condensation or altocumulus wisp was read like a hurricane warning: What if the eclipse were happening *now*? Was Baja California the wrong choice? As the cosmologist lectured on dark matter, his listeners looked up and gasped: a flock of pelicans shadowed the parachute in a primeval wedge. At day's end, campers hauled their folding chairs to the dune's edge to learn how to watch sunsets. Reddening is really the elimination of blue; rays diverge to rejoin behind you like railroad tracks; the earth's rotation creates the daily solar eclipse we call night. Our spinning globe kept people riveted to their seats, scouring the sunset for the green flash, naming the first planets. By dark, people clustered to learn the stars along the ecliptic while others, their tents near telescopes, fell asleep to such phrases as "You're looking back thirty million years in time . . ."

We were also riveted to our seats because we were afraid of losing them. Each person had been issued a folding aluminum chair on arrival, but we were unused to hauling seats from tent to lecture to feeding area and many of us conscripted the nearest empty. Victims began personalizing chairs with luggage tags, then with binoculars and cameras, and it was a tribute either to trust or to inverted values that people used thousand-dollar optics to claim ten-dollar furniture. Musical chairs became a comic subplot and some suspected the staff of subtracting chairs for sport. One man made the mistake of boasting that he was sitting in a heisted chair. "I brought these chairs here," snapped the other, glaring, "and you're sitting in *mine.*"

In our diversity we seemed a more balanced, less erratic group than I'd imagined, and I asked Robert Fadal, one of the two resident doctors, whether we were as healthy as we seemed. We were. There was concern over small things: people got suntan lotion in their eyes; they complained of jellyfish stings with no welts to show for it. "I brought medicine for heart attacks but no tweezers for pulling cactus spines." Despite the vigor of his charges, Dr. Fadal was the most traumatized member of the Centerline staff. Five minutes after his arrival, a fifty-five-year-old man from Rancho Leonero showed up trembling, sweating and saying, "Doctor, I don't feel good." Fadal took him to the infirmary that had been slapped together, ruled out heart attack, stroke and other life threateners, and concluded it was only panic at being far from medical care. Walking him back to Rancho Leonero, Fadal encountered a hulking man with fuzzy eyes and slurred speech that emanated from the back of his mouth. Fadal was reminded of Frankenstein's monster and learned from an employee that the man had beaten up another guest the previous day. There had also been an unidentified streaker in the night. How, wondered Fadal, had so many borderline cases wound up at the same resort? Eventually he learned that the ranch had been struck by a group of rich psychiatric patients who routinely traveled together, apparently unattended. Into this turmoil arrived a young man who had recently been diagnosed with lymphoma, had spent all his money beating it, had hitched to the eclipse, wound up at Leonero and spent most of his time cornering other guests and telling them how good it was to be alive. Dr. Fadal described him as obtrusive, hypersexual and right at home.

LONG BRACED FOR, nearly dreaded, July 11 dawned free of the least blemish. At breakfast all were handed postcard-sized cardboard with insets of an aluminum-coated plastic called Mylar through which we could safely stare at the sun. Hesitantly, watching neighbors for signs of blindness, we put them to our eyes. The sun was a pale bulb. Many began pacing the dune, calculating the optimum viewing spot. Those with tele-scopes that ran on electricity triple-checked the cord from the dune to the generator, as well as the generator. A man who had set up in the cactus for an unobstructed view could be heard cursing his tripods, along with the country that made them. In the midst of scrambling and fussing there was a cheer like the stroke of New Year's. The moon had bitten the sun, on time to the nanosecond.

What followed seemed like bits of a tribal dream. People laid the spread fingers of one hand over the other, creating a mesh through which light fell onto bedsheets in a lattice of crescents. Shadows crispened, cast by a shrinking sun. Three men in blue uniforms, with semiautomatic rifles over their shoulders, suddenly materialized on the dune and strode through the darkening sky watchers. Refusing at first to iden-tify themselves, they admitted under pressure that they were from the Mexican navy. I asked one why they had come. "To protect you," he said. "From what?" I asked. He didn't answer. "From theft?" I persisted. "Yes, from theft during the eclipse." Given that any serious thief would come in the night rather than during the six-minute dusk of the eclipse, and that all of us had been using expensive equipment to nail down cheap seats, the military guard added the traditional spice of the irrational—missing from the Centerline Camp if not from Rancho Leonero—and if I had thought of it in time, I would have asked one of the patrol to guard my folding chair. Invited to peer through lenses and to pose with the more glamorous staff members, they lightened up. All had been warned against taking flash photos that would disrupt night vision, but I nei-ther realized how dark it had become nor remembered my cheap camera's automatic flash, and my blast was answered by a volley of threats. The mountains to the north darkened swiftly, as if under thunderclouds, but without the blackness and screams I had read about in Annie Dillard.

Another cheer went up, followed by a hush: totality had begun. It was now safe to look directly at the sun, yet out of instinct I still hesitated. Soon every naked eye saw the whole moon, opaque as a manhole cover, blot the whole sun, which flowed in blond streamers. After the slow, relentless advance toward darkness, motion stopped. The horizon in all directions glowed melon-pale. However anticipated, it was suddenly stunning that the sun and moon, each a mere 360th of the visible sky, had achieved a cosmic bull's-eye, giving a sense of the clock stopped at a high noon that was midnight. Orion, an impossible sight in July, wobbled behind the sun.

A man stood back from his telescope and cried, "Look at the prominences. Line up and look, but look *quickly.*" Through flares like angels' wings a filament of purple tungsten shot out and halfway back like a varicose vein—or so people afterward, trying to describe it, compounded their metaphors. The coastal resort of Buena Vista sparkled to the north, its light sensors tricked by the dark, and during the middle of totality two dune buggies roared down the beach with the headlights on. While some chattered compulsively and others scurried between instruments, some lay hushed on their backs. A dozen people shouted at once, "Don't look!" Dilated, about to be struck, this was the eyes' one moment of peril. Time ceased stopping, a third cheer went up, and light thin as neon brought back the desert.

After the slow dimming into the eclipse, the equally slow, symmetrical return to full sunlight seemed swift. The gangly pianist danced through the gazers like a crane, blurting impressions from one person to another regardless of who heard what and without slowing his gait. Exhilaration became relief, and crying, "It's Corona time!" many raced to the bar and the parachute silk. At the university in La Paz researchers were still at their posts, but before the moon had freed the sun, the dune was nearly abandoned and the postmortems had begun.

"I had to go to the bathroom during the partial," said one woman, "and light through the straw roof made hundreds of little crescent suns on the toilet seat." A man with a thermometer reported a seventeen-degree drop in temperature. Another couldn't handle his camera, felt his hand paralyze on the shutter, and compared the effect to the rapture of the deep. Replied another, "I had so many straps around my neck, I think my rapture was oxygen deprivation." Someone had heard on the radio that Hawaii was socked in, and I pictured the *Times* reporters in La Paz, giddy with schadenfreude. I asked one of the cosmologists why Dillard's shadow had been more dramatic than ours. "Her eclipse was at daybreak to the north," he said, "while we saw it at noon on the Tropic of Cancer. We got more light from the corona." Unknown to the dune people, a foal was born that afternoon at the ranch behind it. It had a crescent moon—or perhaps a crescent sun—on its forehead and was named, inevitably, Eclipse.

The beach camp unwound through days of snorkeling and sunburn, and I stayed for a day of it. I hiked the beach south toward the little town of La Ribera, past the lagoon where horses were still feeding on underwater weeds as I had first seen them in 1968. Noticing a crowd of people at a large building and thinking it might be a public establishment where I could get a beer, I walked up to find a group of Americans and Mexicans standing around in a sour mood. I slipped away without asking questions and later learned from Dr. Fadal that a retired American man had just died of a massive heart attack while trying to move furniture at noon into his new beach house. Knowing there were doctors at the Centerline Camp, a family member picked them up in a dune buggy and raced them to the house, where they pronounced the man dead. It would take two or three days of paperwork before the body could be flown to the States, with nothing to do but to lay him in the shade under a tarp.

Dr. Fadal also had a curious post-eclipse visit from the senior astronomer, who had signaled when it was safe to watch and when danger returned. He had crescent burns, as if from tiny branding irons, on both retinas and had lost some vision. "Isn't that a particularly dumb thing for an *astronomer* to do?" I asked.

"No, I admire him for it," said Dr. Fadal. "Those are honorable battle scars."

WHEN I RETURNED to La Paz, one story overwhelmed all others: the visit of the Japanese. The 360 visitors consisted of hobbyists and semiprofessionals of an astronomy club led by a tour company that had contracted with Baja Expeditions. All the amenities were ready, and when the nuns refused to allow alcohol in the convent, Tim had backed a truck to their refrigeration room in the middle of the night and stashed the beer behind the soft drinks. The Japanese arrived in an anxious mood because their charter flight had been delayed by a cracked windshield. Baja Expeditions' guide Andrew Davidson, fluent from living for three years in Japan, accompanied the group from the moment they landed at the airport and heard one of their own guides apologize for the bad road into town. When a visitor remarked that the road, which is paved and smooth, wasn't so bad, the guide said, "But the rest of the streets are *terrible*."

Although two-thirds of the group had beds in other hotels, all spent the night awake at the convent, determining which among them deserved the view from the roof. They convened in the chapel. Everything in Japan, said Andrew, even an astronomy club, was a hierarchy, and the most important people, by cosmic necessity, would see more of the eclipse. Most club members had brought telescopes with trackers plus still cameras and video equipment, and they determined that each person needed two square meters. The most important people picked what they deemed the prime spots, then voices rose in contention over how to allocate roof sites among the rest. For a moment Tim couldn't place where he had heard that shouting before, then realized it was a cockfight. At one point the nuns asked a staff person to remind them that they were in a house of God and to please pipe down. Tim was called in to arbitrate, and as soon as he began to speak the voices dropped to an eerie silence as his advice emerged from the interpreter. Tim suggested a lottery. It was held. Winners selected spots next to the elite and losers wound up on an adjacent basketball court. Andrew, because he wasn't Japanese, was not welcome on the roof. Choice vantage points were so important that those who didn't get them were suddenly failures in life. The irony, said Andrew, was that all views were equally good and the Japanese were imposing a rigid power structure on an egalitarian event. Losers on the basketball court, for that matter, would see changes in the colors of the leaves that the elite on the roof would miss.

In the midst of the tension over where to watch fell the long-planned evening meal. The touring company had asked for a barbecue and the nuns didn't want burning fat splattering the garden and the cloister. In an exchange of faxes, Tim realized that the Japanese wanted a fantasy Mexican meal, which appeared to be meat revolving on a spit over leaping flames. He borrowed a rotisserie motor from a street stand, rigged it to his grill, precooked the meat and skewered it over wood doused in diesel fuel. As the meat spun, fat fell to the flames, spurring them higher, and smoke floated into the chapel, where the Japanese were still bickering over how to split up the roof. When the lottery was over, all got a taste of the beef, but the Japanese had expected—or the tour company had led them to expect—that each of the 360 visitors would enjoy a steak-sized cut, not bites to roll in tortillas. Said Andrew, they wanted traditional Mexican food, wanted a cow on a spit, and had confused Mexico with Texas. A woman with the tour company told him, "Your word is your word, it's a matter of honor. Either you provide us with beef or you get us a private beach with shade and drinks for viewing the eclipse."

Tim was summoned to the convent and presented with the ultimatum: a shady beach or beef for 360. He tugged on his mustache, hemmed for time, then promised beef. The eve of the eclipse was a poor night for shopping, but he returned with five kilos of taco meat and presented it to the directors.

"No," they said, "we want to *see beef cooking*."

Tim said to Maria Eugenia, "Where can we can find three hundred kilos of meat tonight?"

Maria Eugenia said, "Tim, it's three in the morning. I hope you're joking."

"They're not," said Tim, "so I'm not."

Tim, Maria Eugenia and another Baja Expeditions employee beat on the doors of butchers, roused them out of their sleep and begged them to sell their entire stock. Tim was determined to hold a grand barbecue for the Japanese after the eclipse. Said Tim, "I want them to eat beef until they pop."

No staff slept that night. They didn't find three hundred kilos of beef, but they did find sixty, in large chunks, which various employees—including Maria Eugenia, who is vegetarian—partially precooked in their homes to lessen the impact on the nuns. In the morning the nuns held a mass that was, in Andrew's words, "very loud, very stagy," and handed out computer printouts saying that the meeting of the sun and moon was the work of God. One female tour guide kept hounding Andrew with questions while blowing cigarette smoke in his face until he threw her out of the kitchen. A few of the Japanese women said to him privately, "I'm so embarrassed, I can't believe people are acting this way." Three of the nuns sneaked up quietly and asked for beer. In their black-and-gray habits and their Mylar glasses for viewing before totality, said Andrew, they looked like tipplers from *Star Trek*.

Shortly before the eclipse, one of the cooks wanted more *machaca* for the impending hors d'oeuvres. Maria Eugenia, seeing an escape from the convent, volunteered, headed to the waterfront and watched the eclipse in the peace of the crowds. Andrew invaded the convent roof and found the Japanese too preoccupied with their equipment to object to his presence. Once the eclipse began, he says, they wholly ignored the square meters they had fought for, melded together, shared equipment, and the whole hierarchical structure dissolved in fraternity.

After the eclipse, every previous problem ceased to exist. The Japanese drank margaritas, laughed, danced, put their arms around each other, loved everyone and hardly noticed they were eating a mere sixty kilos worth of beef. Nuns joined them in downing margaritas. Group pictures were snapped. When they were finally bused back to the plane, everyone who had served them was so exhausted that it seemed barely credible that the Japanese had spent only twenty-two hours in La Paz.

Maria Eugenia's immediate reaction was to quit taking Japanese lessons from Andrew; she didn't want to learn another word. The Japanese, she concluded, were anti-American and she, though Mexican, had been treated as an American. Japanese don't hate Americans, countered Andrew; a foreigner is a foreigner and they dismiss them all equally. Looking back on the event, both concluded that the tour guides, wanting to turn the eclipse into a production starring themselves, were the actual villains, while members of the astronomy club were mostly decent people, merely wound up. When a few of them sent Maria Eugenia souvenir photos of their visit, she resumed her study of Japanese.

As for La Paz itself, one of its more clever preparations had been to declare the eclipse the theme of the preceding Carnaval, enabling the town to save the floats and run them through again on the three nights before the event, with Miss Eclipse waving in a white gown from her pyramid of solar flames. On the great day a fair crowd gathered at the waterfront, with a mob in front of the Hotel La Perla cheering and applauding, and it was said that as the temperature plunged during totality, there was a quick and pungent smell of the sea. A woman in back of town reported that during the eclipse all dogs, children and roosters alike fell silent; then when the sun emerged, the roosters began to crow. One family watched their neighbors stand outside during the partial eclipse, then pile into the house and bolt the door during the totality, when it was safe to look. Several people reported neighbors who tied red ribbons around their trees to keep the fruit from rotting and the trees themselves from dying, including a woman who proceeded to kill the same trees next month with an overdose of fertilizer. Tim, who climbed above the most elite of the Japanese to watch from the convent bell tower, described the eclipse as a compressed sunset. Doves returned to the tower to roost, spotted him and swerved back to the penumbra. His attention was torn between strange sights in the sky and strange sounds from the roof, where the Japanese were saying *whoa* and *ooh* and emitting low guttural rumblings that he took for darker versions of *wow*. The winemaker watched with friends in his backyard menagerie, where his rabbits ate more furiously and his doves went back to sleep. He also said that he created a cocktail called the Eclipse, compounded of brandy and his damiana liqueur, producing a private eclipse in whoever drank it. "Downing those," I asked, "how could you tell *what* your animals were doing?"

"We saved them for after the eclipse," he said, fluttering his eyebrows. "One blackout at a time."

The last minute held a last surprise, a chartered DC-10 from Salt Lake City that landed at the La Paz airport at three in the morning before the event, disgorging two hundred people with sleeping bags, lawn chairs, scopes, cameras and no plans at all. When they headed with their gear over the nearest barbed-wire fence in the dark, airport officials became alarmed that they would impale themselves on the cholla and directed them to a nearby soccer field. The Utahns calmly set up, watched the eclipse unobstructed and boarded their plane back to Salt Lake at four the next afternoon.

As for the dreaded Woodstock of astronomy, it never happened. There was actually less traffic than during Carnaval, a purely local event. A tour of the gift shops showed little dent in the ashtrays and T-shirts, and indeed I bought my own souvenir eclipse mug the following winter. A man who had invested his savings in Mylar to sell during the eclipse lost all when the Mexican government, without advance notice, passed out free Mylar to protect the eyes of its citizens. Of the businesses named for the eclipse that I encountered, the Palapa Eclipse in San Ignacio lasted only a season but the Eclipse Disco in Ciudad Constitución, Eclipse Purified Water in La Paz, and '91 Eclipse Honey became lingering concerns. Almost no one patronized the government tent cities at sixty dollars a night, and no one who rented a house to eclipse watchers is known to have paid a tax or offered it for government inspection. An official visitor count was never published, but the braced-for half million is thought to have been somewhere between thirty thousand and fifty thousand. The millennial tradition of anticipating calamities was thus maintained. Instead of earthquakes and invasion, people projected the more contemporary fears of roadblocks, running out of gas and not finding a motel room for the night.

As for the eclipse itself, a year and a half after the event I asked Dr. Fadal how it struck him. "I frankly wasn't interested in the actual eclipse," he said, "and couldn't see what the fuss was about. I came because it was something different to do as a doctor. Then totality began and here was the most pure, penetrating, all-encompassing, magnanimous, black, engulfing, sucking thing, which was surrounded by"—and here he began to hiss—"this sssearing sssilver ssstrip, with these little chartreuse daggers sticking into it and this—whauw!—wispy aurora on either side six hundred million miles, and you're looking at this thing and thinking that it has absolutely nothing to do with you. It doesn't care if there's a perception to perceive it, it's just a phenomenon, but it gives you faith that there's beauty in the world."

The same winter I asked Andrew, who defied the Japanese on the convent roof, how it affected him. "It was like, like . . ." He groped for a sufficient metaphor. "It was like intravenous poetry."

IN THE WINTER OF 1973, as the rain pounded and the critically ill Brandy and I burned ironwood to stay warm, more than bright weather I craved a consoling piano. I had played since I was eight, had ingested the classical repertoire and could fake the popular styles. My three-year nightclub career in Andalucía taught me that the piano was a good passport to a country's interior. In 1973 I was more interested in soothing my own interior than in penetrating La Paz, but I had gazed with curiosity at a one-story building of rough-hewn *cantera* on one corner of the plaza. Labeled *Escuela de Música*, it could hardly be a music school without a piano.

One morning I stepped through the open door and found myself in a room of cool bare walls, utterly silent. Perhaps their day had not yet begun. Through the shadows gloomed an original painting of Schumann, his eyebrows like scrolls over a

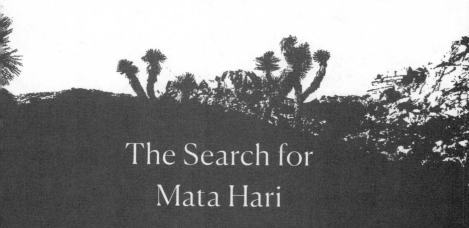

The Search for
Mata Hari

deep mad gaze, lost in the manic phase of his schizophrenia. From another room came a sound of sweeping. Open doorways gave in two directions and I advanced toward the broom. It was wielded by a boy in his teens. "Buenos días," I said.

He jumped. "Buenos días."

I explained that I was a visitor in search of a piano: was there one in the school I might practice on? There were two, he said, but I would have to ask the *profesora*, who wouldn't arrive until later.

I returned at eleven. The front room was still empty but sounds of a keyboard and voices rose from the interior. I passed through a small room containing a single glass cabinet with a few stringed instruments and reached a third room with a middle-aged woman, a Yamaha console piano and two girls of about eleven. I excused myself for interrupting and explained my presence. The woman introduced herself as Consuelo Amador de Ribera. She did not seem startled by my request and explained that she was teaching a piece she particularly liked. Would I like to hear it?

I would indeed.

She played a mid-nineteenth-century salon piece, a little stiffly but with strong left-hand octaves I envied. I squinted at the score and didn't recognize the composer. When she finished, I told her I admired her octaves.

"Really?" She seemed genuinely pleased. "But now you play something."

There is an intermezzo by Schumann with a singing melody and a rolling bass that falls easily under the fingers, which I have trained myself to discharge amid most states of panic, inebriation or absence of practice, and I discharged it. I turned around to apologize for the wooden fingers and found the *profesora* staring wide-eyed. "But this is wasted on just the three of us," she said. "I'm trying to teach a history of music course in the afternoon but I don't have any examples. You must come back tomorrow and let me tape some music."

It was clear that I was not going to sit down and practice, but flushed with the idea of recording, I promised to return tomorrow at the same time.

The next morning I was greeted by Consuelo, two colleagues on the faculty and some forty children ranging in age from six to late teens. Consuelo introduced me to the other two adults, then asked me to play. Not to repeat the Schumann, I played a couple of pieces by Brahms. During the applause I looked in vain for a tape recorder.

"Our problem here," said Consuelo, "is that the government gives us this large building and our small salaries but no equipment. As you see, we have almost no furniture. We have this console, an upright in another room, and what the students can provide themselves. Do you think it might be possible to play a benefit concert for us, so we could raise some money?"

To be an international concert pianist was a lifetime dream whose possibility suddenly struck terror. Yet when would I be asked again? If I came apart, no one I knew would find out. Even Brandy couldn't attend. "I don't know how long I'll be here," I said. "I could be leaving as soon as next week."

"Then we'd better try for this weekend. How's Saturday?"

It was Tuesday. That would mean only five days of preparation, five days of dread. "Saturday would be fine."

"And what are you going to play?"

Now I was truly off guard. "I'd need a day to figure that out." At this point anyone who mistook me for a concert pianist should have wondered at my not having a choice of programs at my fingertips, but Consuelo merely answered, "We don't have a day. If we're going to put this on by Saturday, we should get the program to the printer this afternoon."

"Then let me think about it and come back in a couple of hours. By the way, who is your favorite composer?"

"Mozart. But I really think any recital should begin with Bach."

I made my escape before I received further instruction.

I stopped by the house to check on Brandy, changed into swimming trunks, grabbed a pencil and notebook, and headed to the beach. The sun poured on my back while my mind raced. I was safest with romantics like Schumann, whom I could blur with overpedaling if I got in trouble, and with moderns that could absorb mistakes in the general dissonance. The delicacy and precision of Mozart was treacherous: Mozart was out. I could pass off Bach with a couple of selections from the French suites, then recover with the Schumann. Next I listed Chopin's Ballade in G Minor, two pieces by Brahms, four preludes by Rachmaninoff, Debussy's *Reflets dans l'eau*, a movement from a Hindemith sonata, the "Sevilla" of Albéniz to touch base with the Spanish repertoire, and concluded with Gershwin's *Rhapsody in Blue*, which I could grandstand to the point of annihilating whatever had preceded it. I added the estimated times: it came to an hour and a half. Nine composers was unprecedented variety, but constant shifts would obscure the deficiencies of any particular style, and with a generous intermission and perhaps a late start it should see me through the evening.

I returned to Consuelo with the lineup. "Estupendo," she proclaimed, ignoring the absence of Mozart.

"Before you take it to the printer," I said, "I'd like to run through it to make sure the length is all right." My actual motive was to assure myself I could get through it at all. We put a stopwatch on the piano, and while children gathered and the temperature spiraled, I plugged away to the end. It was just an hour and a half.

Consuelo was grinning. "Now," she said, "I need to know something of your training and career so I can get going on the publicity."

I told her that I had studied at Yale, that I had performed for three years in Spain as well as variously in the United States, that I had played for a theater company and for Ballet West. I did not tell her that I merely took lessons on the side while pursuing a degree in English, that in Spain I had played only restaurants and nightclubs, that the theater company was performing a melodrama called *The Drunkard*, that for Ballet West I ground out exercise classes, that my American career consisted of private parties, silent films and one counterculture funeral. I never directly lied but was judicious with the truth.

"There is another problem," I said, "which is that I didn't expect to be performing and don't have anything formal to wear." My wardrobe, in fact, consisted of plaid shirts and jeans, with a choice of hiking boots, sandals or sneakers.

"No problem," she said, "we should be able to borrow a suit and shoes. We have several students your size."

"Since this is a benefit, if you get anything from a store, make them donate it. Don't spend any money . . ."

"You do the music," she said, "and I'll handle the rest."

"One more thing. I can't remember some of the opus numbers for the program."

"We'll look up what we can."

Next morning I bought the papers to see if the publicity had started. I found myself on the front page of one and the third page of another, an international concert star with an extensive career in the United States and Europe, possessed of golden hands, magic fingers, the kind of paraphernalia thought to have been buried with Liszt. I proceeded to the music school to start practicing. The energetic Consuelo met me with a suit jacket from a tailor down the street who rented clothes, primarily to ranchers who attended city weddings. It was a small and hideous black-and-white checked affair that bound me like a cobra. The first cross-hand passage would surely split the back. "No," recoiled Consuelo, to my relief, "that will never do."

"Can't you borrow something from a student?"

"Leave it to me."

Next was the matter of the piano. The concert was to be held at the back end of town, in La Casa de la Juventud, a primary-school auditorium supposedly equipped with a baby grand. I drove us out there to test it. The action veered from the shrill to the nonfunctional and the instrument was, in concert parlance, a piano-shaped object. "What else is there?"

"The two at the school." That meant the dysfunctional upright or the Japanese console, a model that was halfway between an upright and a spinet.

"Then it's the console."

On Thursday morning I found that Consuelo had assembled a full suit of clothes, including a well-fitted blue blazer, trousers, tie, and a white shirt and loafers in boxes from a store. "I hope you didn't *buy* the shirt and shoes," I said.

"Will you leave those details to me?" She then told me that the concert had been plugged constantly on radio and TV and was now nearly sold out.

The government had reserved the first three rows in a block. "And you have a live interview on television tomorrow, just after the evening news."

"Incidentally," I suddenly asked, "have any other visiting pianists played in La Paz?"

"No, you're the first."

The next day I got in some practice and studied the press clippings so as not to say anything that might conflict with my official career. In the evening I got into my blue blazer and drove out to the TV station, a small building on a hill over the bay. The sensations came so fast I had little time to panic. A pair of announcers under punishingly bright lights traded dispatches, international politics followed by local crimes. One of them then informed the viewers that they were in for a special privilege, an interview with an internationally known concert pianist. He got up and gave me his seat.

To sit in someone else's clothes, blinded by lights, and account for a fictional self in another language gave me a burst of confidence. I was asked where I was trained and where I had played, and replied with the information I had given Consuelo. When I mentioned what I was going to play, the announcer said, "Well, that sounds like a very melodic, very popular program," suggesting a suspicious knowledge of music. The interview, which I'm told lasted five minutes, seemed over the instant it began.

The morning of the concert I woke at dawn and faced a long day of anxiety. Mid-morning I drove to the plaza, parked, and walked toward the post office. A pickup with the piano pulled up to the light as I waited to cross. It was the perfect diversion. I hailed the students riding with the piano and jumped into the truck just as the light changed. As the truck pulled away, I tumbled toward the street, the students grabbed me, and but for split-second timing I might have ended my apprehension with a broken arm.

We parked at the back of the auditorium and were supervised by a woman who seemed baffled by my presence. "Do you have a ticket to tonight's performance?" she asked.

"Well, no," I said, taken aback.

"Then I'm afraid you can't come," she shrugged. "It's sold out."

Inside I found Consuelo attending to the decoration of the stage. The piano was to sit on one side, balanced on the other by the manic portrait of Schumann propped on an easel between sprays of white gladiolas, glaring as if to say, you will enjoy this concert or else. Until now I had greeted every detail like a rapt spectator, but now that I was a *concertista internacional*, surely I could indulge my moment of temperament. Schumann, I informed Consuelo, had to go.

"¿Pero por qué?"

"Because," I said, hardly knowing where to begin, "he just isn't right."

I arrived well before concert time, to find most of the audience already seated. From the wings I could see that the stage itself was lined with folding chairs, several deep, and the air was already dense and steamy. I glanced at the program. The Chopin Ballade in G Minor was listed as opus 4. "I looked it up," said Consuelo. I knew that the Ballade had been written in Paris, that Chopin didn't get out of Poland until well after opus 10, and that the number couldn't be right. Admission, I noted, was ten pesos, about seventy cents. It was 8:30. "Shouldn't we begin?" I asked Consuelo. She ignored the suggestion. I kept thinking that in a couple of hours I would be on my way to the banquet they were throwing afterward. However I played, I was soon headed toward food and drink. My heart hammered, but with a fatalistic calm.

At five minutes of nine the houselights flashed. I handed Consuelo my glasses, less for cosmetic reasons than to blur the audience, and like a first-time parachuter I walked out of the wings, through the folding chairs, past gladiolas bereft of Schumann, and bowed toward a mist of applause. The first few measures would determine it all. I raised my hands over a G major chord and began. I was answered by Bach, inexpressive but without a hitch. When I reached the end of the first piece there was applause, which I hadn't expected until I finished the Bach selection. There was nothing to do but stand up and acknowledge it. I got through the rest of the Bach, bowed again, and dove into the Schumann with a flourish. From here to the end it was a matter of sheer perseverance and remembering what I was supposed to play next.

As I got used to the occasion, the playing loosened and I began to take in my surroundings. It was hot and getting hotter; it was easily eighty-five degrees. The entire audience seemed to be coughing. The flu had been sweeping La Paz—I was to come down with it the following week—and the more I listened, the more the hall sounded like a hospital. There were, in addition, children of all ages, many of them with me onstage, many of them whispering and playing furtive games. The distraction might have ruffled a career performer, but I have always played better when someone was running the vacuum or arguing in another room, and the clatter had a tonic effect.

In practicing the music, however, I had forgotten the nakedest moment of all: the bow. Scheduling so many short pieces for an audience inclined to applaud every cadence, there were many, many bows. When the piece ended I would stand up with my left hand on the piano, as I was once taught, make a forward nod from the waist, hold the position a moment and do it again if the noise didn't stop. After the first three or four of those maneuvers I could hear a snickering, slightly more public each time. Why hadn't I practiced in front of a mirror? Did I dare experiment with it now?

I bowed for intermission and escaped backstage. Consuelo

was jubilant. I talked little and tried to sustain an inner momentum. Drinks were an hour away. The four Rachmaninoff preludes were next. To avoid bowing for each I extended my palm like a traffic cop, glared at the blur over the piano and recommenced. Soon I was through the Hindemith, through the Albéniz, and ready to plunge into the *Rhapsody in Blue*. I gunned the pedal, flung my arms, and gave a rendition my more candid friends refer to as "The Killing of Sister George." I made a last wooden bow into sustained applause and fled backstage. It was over.

The applause continued. "They want an encore," whispered Consuelo, prodding my arm. Was this never to end? After the *Rhapsody* it would have to be something quiet and simple. I played the first section of Chopin's Étude in E. The audience collectively sighed. I stopped where it comes to a cadence, before the pyrotechnic middle, stood up and bowed once more.

When I was backstage and the audience was at last filing out, Consuelo asked, "Why didn't you play the rest of the étude?"

"It's not under my fingers at the moment."

"Anyway, they all knew the melody, since they used it on TV for a tissue commercial."

But not all the audience left. A fair crowd had gathered around the stage to have their programs signed, mostly children, with a couple of middle-aged women who gushed and raved. When their demands were met, we piled into cars and headed to the banquet.

El Yate was the most exclusive restaurant in La Paz, but my dreams of eating there had only gone as far as fresh lobster and hadn't imagined a dinner in my honor. A U-shaped table awaited, glittering with silver and white napery. Consuelo and I presided at the center, flanked by people Consuelo identified as local officials, parents of students, financial contributors and assorted relatives. I ate copiously, drank all that appeared in my glass, and was gnawed by a lingering doubt. What if some reporter knew the difference between overpedaling and clean playing? What if I was unmasked in the morning papers? I asked Consuelo whether any critics might be reviewing the event.

"Oh, yes," she said brightly, "they're here with us tonight."

"Which are they?" I asked in fright. When she pointed to the two gushy ladies who had asked for photographs, I knew I was home free.

In the morning I stopped by the music school to return the suit and find out how much they had made from the concert. At ten pesos a head they had netted almost three hundred dollars, indicating an audience of about four hundred. "We had to buy the shirt and shoes," admitted Consuelo, handing them back, "so please keep them as a gift." I assumed that the spotlight had passed, but for days afterward people came up to me on the street, or detained me as I cashed a traveler's check, or collared me as I bought potatoes, to tell me they especially liked the Brahms or the Debussy. I still felt I had acted out a fantasy, but if people took me for the real thing, was I the deceived? La Paz struck me as unturned soil where anything artistic, or at least musical, might grow.

I watched for the reviews. I never found anything by either of the ladies, but I did discover one of some length by a man whose name was unfamiliar. He praised the precision of the Bach, the delicacy of the Debussy, the vigor of the Gershwin, then denounced the hair in the musical soup—the wretched behavior of the children and the failure of parents to control them. I bought the last copy on the stand, then rushed from store to store looking for more. I ran into an acquaintance who asked why I was dashing about with so little dignity. When I explained, he told me the reviewer was a close friend and he would conduct me to him. I found myself in a newspaper office talking to a man in his mid-thirties from Mexico City, a veteran of many concerts who was stuck in the provinces and sincerely liked the performance.

And there the episode would have ended but for a strange coda. A few days later I received a call from a woman named Quichu Isaïs. She belonged to a faction that had split from Consuelo and had rallied around an old and distinguished composer who had written, among other things, the official Baja California Sur state song, "Costa Azul." Luis Peláez had been the music school's first director and had taught there until Consuelo, they claimed, kicked him out. They couldn't be seen at any function arranged by Consuelo, but neither did they want to miss the visiting pianist. Quichu would be so grateful if I would go some morning to the composer's house and repeat the performance for him and a few friends . . . Was this a musical tar baby from which I would never be free? I couldn't imagine anyone not liking the gracious and lively Consuelo, but what did I know about La Paz intrigue?

I met Quichu at her home near the waterfront and rode with her to the composer's house. I asked about the rift between the composer and Consuelo. It was a scandal, she said. He had taught Consuelo music, hired her to teach at the school, then put her in charge and she fired him.

A silver-haired, ruddy-faced man in his sixties met us at the door. Instead of shaking my hand he took them both in his, inspected them as if estimating karats and pronounced, "We must take advantage of genius when it comes along." I nearly broke out in a cold sweat.

In the room were a half-dozen people, including two nuns with a tape recorder. I accepted coffee, then asked the composer about his music. Was any of it recorded? Could I hear some? He said that he had never gotten around to copyrighting it, was afraid someone would steal it, and therefore kept it to himself. He would, however, play some for me. He played a couple of fast character pieces, of mild syncopation and dissonance, then announced he would play his personal favorite, called "Mata Hari, or the Bird of Morning."

"Mata Hari, the spy?" I asked.

"There is the delusion. People think she was a spy, but I have read all the books and sifted the evidence. She was innocent and she was martyred. I have written her music." He turned around, and over a bass of sevenths, with a melody colored by grace notes a fifth above, he picked out an obsessively reharmonized phrase that called up some ravishing slow movement from Villa-Lobos.

"Could I hear it again?" I asked. He obliged.

I knew that my moment was fast approaching. The composer excused himself and went to the kitchen. Under a clock that now read 10:30 I saw him pour a stiff splash of what looked like Kentucky bourbon into a tumbler, toss it off, steady himself a moment, then return. Might that have been a factor in his dismissal? The composer resettled in his armchair, one of the nuns punched on the recorder and I lit into the trusty Schumann. I played a few more pieces without trying to repeat the entire program. As a gesture toward the composer's own heritage I concluded with the "Sevilla," which trails off in diminishing chords and ends with a final chord that should blaze like a gong. I have learned since to place my hands over the keys and snap my wrists so that the chord rings true as the hands fly up, but at the time I knew only to swoop upon it like a hawk. I missed.

I was the only one to laugh. The rest applauded politely and the nuns switched off the recorder. I asked the composer if I could have a copy of "Mata Hari." No, he said sadly, he couldn't risk having it pirated. I rose to go, urging him to get his work copyrighted so it could be heard. He urged me to keep playing and, in the episode's most truthful moment, to find more time to practice.

On the way back Quichu said she had been trying for years to get the composer even to write down his work so that she could copyright it but, she sighed, he was basically lazy. I left La Paz with an image of a public hungry for music and a small musical community at each other's throats.

OVER THE NEXT seventeen years I kept marginally in touch with music in La Paz. I, too, was haunted by Mata Hari—the music, not the spy—and in 1975 I knocked on the composer's door. He greeted me warmly and asked me in. I told him how much I had admired "Mata Hari." Would he play it for me? When he finished, I asked again for a copy of the score. He was so afraid it would be plagiarized, he said, that he hadn't even committed it to staff paper. In that case, would he play it again? He did, and I asked to hear it one more time. Pleased, he repeated it as I ran my mental recording system. If I could hear it a few more times, I thought, I could capture it, but to ask for it again was awkward. The music itself was elusive, and when I left the house it vanished like a dream that melts as one reaches for it.

When I returned to La Paz in 1977, a friend drove me to the music school's new location on a street off the plaza. Consuelo was bustlingly in charge but the quarters were cramped and no better equipped. Consuelo asked me to play, and in front of a dozen students I attempted Chopin's Ballade no. 3, which had been well under control before I left home. Half blind and stiff after weeks without playing, I slaughtered it. When I inquired after Luis Peláez, the composer, I learned he had died, presumably taking "Mata Hari" with him.

In the early eighties I learned that the music school had acquired its own campus, and I pulled up to the orange iron fence endemic to state-run schools. I walked dumbstruck into a complex of long, elegant buildings landscaped with hibiscus, oleander, almond and rubber trees. I found the office and asked for Consuelo. A secretary told me she was in conference; would I please be seated. Consuelo, ten minutes later, was friendly but harried and offered me a quick tour. There were rows of practice rooms, classrooms and a small auditorium, all surrounded by immaculate foliage. I recognized the Yamaha console and saw that the mad portrait of Schumann was part of a series that included Beethoven and Bach. How had all this sprung into being? It was, said Consuelo, a conjunction of luck. A man who had studied eight years with the music school became governor and allocated funds for the campus. When the buildings were up but empty, Carmen de López Portillo, wife of the Mexican president José López Portillo, came through La Paz and Consuelo staged a concert in her honor. Señora López Portillo was so impressed that a month later the necessary instruments arrived—pianos, guitars, violins, violas and cellos. Meanwhile, the school had snared a Brazilian pianist who had studied for five years in Vienna and was the new star of the faculty. Consuelo's five minutes for me were up and I left awed by the music school's turn of fortune.

. . .

WHEN I RETURNED to spend entire winters in La Paz in the early nineties, I approached the new music school as I had once approached the old one off the plaza, a bit intimidated, suffering piano withdrawal and craving practice. Consuelo had retired, but the new director told me I was welcome to play weekday mornings—quiet time before schools let out and children poured in for lessons. The school became a daily routine during which I drilled under the gaze of Schumann or Bach and rested my eyes out the window, where a woman cleaned and a man hosed and gardened, gossiping excitedly, and another man, idle and silent, paraded through the courtyard making sure nothing was amiss.

Since the morning students were all adults with their own pianos, I was the only regular who used the rooms strictly for practice. Iberê, the Brazilian teacher, was bearded, detached, humorous, a virtuoso with an eye for irony. Among his students were Alejandrina the veterinarian, full of well-focused enthusiasm; Fernando, a young man who owned a shoe store; Lupe, who sought refuge in the piano from her socially prominent family; Iliana, a university student; Maricela, who had an aquarium concession at Alejandrina's clinic; and assorted housewives. The string instruments that Consuelo had received from Señora López Portillo were in storage and I never saw one. Aside from an occasional drummer through the wall and a couple of guitarists and a brass band on Fridays, the school was purely a piano school. Classical concerts by the school were piano solos, piano duets or duo piano. During my first winter at the school I was invited to participate in a duo piano recital with Iberê and his students.

The occasion was the school's fiftieth anniversary, for it had been founded in 1942, in a location previous to the one on the plaza. I was keen on the piece—a Busoni transcription of Mozart's overture to *The Magic Flute*—and still more eager for the social events that surrounded the concert. The first of these, whose object was to make plans, was convened at Alejandrina's veterinary clinic.

It surprised me that the music school and the venues around town, all staffed by ample bureaucracies, left the performers to design programs, make and distribute posters, print and sell tickets. I had attended the inauguration of the city's landmark hall, the Teatro de la Ciudad, in 1986. Notables included the president of Mexico, Miguel de la Madrid, and I had been struck by the casualness with which his small entourage passed while people stood in silence. A young man in our party gave a yip like a bored coyote, saying afterward that it was, after all, the president and somebody should do something. The hall was large and architecturally impressive, but the grand piano that accompanied the popular program thudded without resonance, hadn't been tuned and was periodically drowned out by a gale-force air conditioner behind us. The air conditioner had since been tempered but the instrument was the same piano-shaped object. Local performers could only rent this imposing hall at exorbitant rates and do all the publicity themselves. Geny Bergold, La Paz's other Brazilian pianist, played a recital there when she first arrived, but despite a respectable house she lost money. To avoid the theater's pitfalls we would be playing the municipal art gallery next door, where the audience would writhe on folding chairs but the musicians would stay in the black.

We met in the back room of the veterinary clinic, a cavernous chamber with a spinet. The adult pianists had become a social group with a name—La Tecla Perpetua, or the Eternal Key—and the standard drink was the *cubano*, a mix of brandy,

Pepsi, club soda and ice, nursed while packs of cigarettes were consumed. We spent a couple of hours over a statement for the program. How, for instance, were we to refer to our audience? The first suggestion, Paceños and Baja Californians, was discarded when we realized that most concertgoers came from elsewhere. The majority were from Mexico City and other urban areas of the interior, with a sprinkling of foreigners that included Americans from the marina. Someone mentioned that a teachers' event conflicted with ours and perhaps we should reschedule. No, came the objection, teachers were paid too little to attend concerts and weren't our target. Alejandrina said she would get the governor to attend because she was veterinarian to his pets. By midnight we had knocked out our three sentences, and each of us then played our half of the duo piano pieces amid enthusiastic comment, though, musically, they made only half-sense.

The evening before the performance we gathered at the gallery to see to the placement of the pianos and to run through the program on-site. Two consoles from the school, one of them the Yamaha I had played nineteen years before, waited next to planking for a stage. We constructed a small platform and angled the pianos just so. As we ran through the pieces we had spent months perfecting, they suddenly sounded hollow and deficient. The echo of our practice room at the school, where the pianos spanned an entire wall, had redoubled the sonority and deceived us. Here the pianos were naked, ill-matched, untuned by the move and lost in the reaches of the gallery. We lacked even a tuner to turn to. All of us were let down, and Iberê, for whom the concert was a momentary focus of his career, railed against incompetence and appeared to be facing the abyss. We opened the piano tops, to no avail. Alejandrina suggested removing the boards under the keys to expose the harplike entrails, and suddenly we felt the vibrations and heard the sonority. We all played better, and though the pianos were still ill-matched and untuned, at least we could make noise for the audience.

At midnight Alejandrina invited us to her clinic, which was just across the street, for *cubas*. Before she could attend us, she had to check on two sick animals. She returned five minutes later to report that the monkey was hanging on but the dog had died. As she was reaching into the ice chest to fill our glasses, she suddenly looked up and said, "I just want you to know that I washed my hands after I disposed of the dead dog." That moment, more than any other, still evokes for me the flavor of classical music in La Paz.

The day of the concert I was again scrambling for suitable clothes. Fernando had lent me a white shirt and black pants, but the waist was too small and at the last minute he had to substitute a pair of his father's, which Alejandrina ironed an hour before starting time. Word-of-mouth and our few posters had filled the chairs, with more attendants lining the walls, menacing the lithographs, and we cut off ticket sales at 150. The governor didn't show and was rumored to have gone to a boxing match instead. Iberê uncorked a bottle of rosé backstage and each of us had a belt before going on to perform. The pre-concert crises must have relaxed us, for we all played our best, drank at the waterfront afterward with fans, then repaired to the veterinary clinic for a celebratory session of La Tecla Perpetua. Deep into the night Iberê disclosed that he was a grandnephew of the soprano Renate Tebaldi. Consuelo's son admitted that what he remembered from my concert in 1973, when he was a nine-year-old, wasn't the music but my Hush Puppies, cool new shoes that had not yet reached La Paz. I wanted to see the evening's revelations to a close but was facing a radio interview the next morning and left at three. I later learned that Iberê, Alejandrina and Fernando philosophized until eight, then went out to breakfast and were spotted, with much amusement, by a doctor who had attended the concert and recognized that the bleary-eyed musicians were still dressed for performance.

IN SUBSEQUENT YEARS of practicing at the school, participating in concerts and socializing with La Tecla Perpetua, I was constantly reminded that Baja California remained a frontier for the arts. The indigenous population had been wiped out and the peninsula resettled by ranchers, fishermen, miners and traders whose concerns were necessarily practical. When they expressed themselves artistically, it was in crafts— in tooled leatherwork for saddles, in intricately strung beads of wood and rawhide. They appropriated the ranch music of northern Mexico, sometimes adding new tunes and local verses. Even the most popular presentation at El Teatro de La Paz, Los Huizapoles—roughly, the Burrs—was a pair of comics who glorified ranching culture by taking it to its extremes in parody. Artistically, La Paz was said to be "behind the Cholla Curtain." Iberê, who eventually left La Paz because of better performing opportunities elsewhere, felt exhilarated by the idea of inscribing classical music on a blank slate. In La Paz one could sell shoes or inoculate cats by day and perform classical music by night. Because Baja California was a cultural desert, those of modest ability—as I had learned some time before— could participate at a higher level than they could where culture was deep-rooted.

But I noticed that older members of the La Paz musical

community didn't think of themselves as pioneers but as having fallen from a golden age. In the thirties and early forties, went their version, La Paz had more grand pianos than cars. Quichu Isaïs, who had summoned me to the old composer's home in 1973 and had since moved to Vienna, told a radio interviewer that pianism in Baja California had started in the small silver-mining town of El Triunfo, south of La Paz, toward the end of the nineteenth century. The leading families were European, with little indigenous blood, and every ranch had two grand pianos, some even three. Playing piano was as natural as breathing, and little girls who stumbled over their Beethoven were admonished, What do you want to do when you grow up, *cook*? Pianists kept up with new European music and the latest scores by Debussy were better known in El Triunfo than they were in Mexico City. With the close of El Triunfo's silver mines, the leading families moved to La Paz and perpetuated the tradition in the form of salons and *tertulias*, weekly get-togethers whose members would recite, stage dramatic works and make music. The founding of the La Paz Music School actually pre-dated Bellas Artes, the famous school in Mexico City. The music school extended the public grade and high school curricula, requiring knowledge of solfeggio, mastery of scales and the performance of difficult music from memory. In a flourish of genealogy, Quichu said that Luis Peláez, founding director of the music school, had studied with Gomez Anda, who studied with Krauze, who studied with Liszt, who studied with Czerny, who studied with Beethoven. Classical music in Baja California came straight from the source.

Iberê was agnostic about La Paz's golden age of music. To hear them talk, he said, you would think El Triunfo and La Paz were Paris and Berlin. Nobody throws away a grand piano, and if there were more of them than cars, where are they now? We don't lack for old cars. Why didn't the old guard perpetuate the golden age instead of waxing nostalgic and blaming the present? Why, for instance, did Quichu move to Vienna—where she met Iberê and dispatched *him* to rescue music in La Paz? Elma Vidaurri, a deodorizer distributor who visited La Paz in the fifties and moved there in the early seventies, confirmed the vitality of the tertulias. The weekly gatherings were anticipated, were exciting, were the heart of La Paz. Most gathering places had pianos, though most of the pianos, she added, were uprights. She ascribed the death of the tertulias to the coming of TV, videos and discos, as well as the swamping of tight-knit groups by new arrivals—a point also made by Quichu in her interview. The older generation felt that La Paz was losing culture rather than gaining it as it grew. Newcomers felt left out.

An instance of cultural decline was made vivid to me one morning by Lupe, descendant of the family that was said to have had the best salon in La Paz. She was desperate to play the piano, even though she had one in her own living room. When she played at home, her husband and even her grown live-in children verbally abused her: why did she have to play that horrible music, that Mozart, that Chopin? Sometimes they went so far as to drown her out with rock radio. She taught at the music school in the afternoon, in a room with her name on the door, and I usually practiced in that room in the morning because it had the best piano. Occasionally she dropped by herself to play and would ask if I would be so kind as to switch to some other room in the few minutes when she could have some peace. I knew through La Tecla Perpetua that her husband's life was a nonstop cabaret, but I was newly shocked that this patriarchal family's insensitivity should reduce this lovely woman to apologizing for her rights. Never did I more eagerly surrender a piano.

If La Paz had fallen from a golden age, what was the evidence in the other arts? The best-known painter in town was Francisco Merino, who had arrived from Mexico City in the early eighties, had created such public art as murals for city hall, modernized cave paintings for the Hotel La Perla, and even the blue shell behind the altar of the Adorers, along with his own easel paintings. For him the only conceivable golden age in the visual arts would be the era of the original cave paintings, whenever that was. But there had been two minor waves of art, the first, between 1950 and 1965, centered around the Escuela Normal, the teachers' college. La Paz was still physically isolated, and its art, reflecting a ranching and fishing culture, tended toward naive landscape painting. In the early seventies, when Baja California Sur became a state, the road was finished, ferry service was in place and the university was founded, the arts received a larger, state-funded impulse. Fishing was already in decline and the government thought that tourism might be boosted by an infusion of art that looked folkloric and indigenous. A group of artists trekked by mule to the mid-peninsula cave paintings, though only Francisco actually incorporated the motifs in his work. Literary magazines surfaced and succumbed at the university. Francisco opened a *peña*—a café where customers could perform verbally and musically, a kind of public tertulia—and kept it open for a couple of years. The university now and then brought out books of scholarship and original poetry. With the election in 1986 of the governor who had chosen boxing over our concert, state funding for the arts came to an end. La Paz lacked even a commercial gallery and anyone who wanted to live by the brush had to go to Cabo San Lucas, with its hotels full of rich foreigners.

Perhaps there had been a golden age of the piano, but even pianists were back to being pioneers.

AS A FOREIGNER in La Paz I enjoyed the pioneering: a request to play for an oceanography class graduation, the offer of a formal recital in the small auditorium of the music school. This latter was a chance, twenty years later, to improve on the concert of 1973, and I scheduled largely the same program. This time I was armed with my own white shirt and black pants and I knew the correct opus numbers of all the pieces. The piano was a new Chinese grand donated to the school by Consuelo, and the hall, with extra chairs, probably held a hundred people. Over my head, instead of the manic portrait of Schumann, was a reproduction of Delacroix's Chopin, my favorite painting of any composer. The ambient temperature was normal, there was little coughing, the children didn't squirm, and I had learned how to bow. I did notice an inordinate amount of whispering between pieces. During intermission I learned that the programs, with their impeccable information and meticulously worded tribute to the music school faculty, had been inadvertently locked in the office, no one had the key, and the audience was trying to figure out what I was playing. I was still pioneering after all, and I announced the rest of the program from the stage.

In 1993 came an unexpected addition to La Paz culture, a café that Nora, wife of Tim Means, opened on the waterfront. To my private delight, it was the very space that had been occupied by El Yate, where the banquet had been held after my concert in 1973. A more elaborate version of the peña that Francisco Merino had tried earlier, the Café Chanate offered beer and wine, cappuccino and light food, views in three directions, and an upright piano. Nora encouraged locals and visitors to try their acts, often sight unseen. I worked up nights of tangos, of Brazilian music and, closest to my heart, an all-Gershwin concert to take place during the Fiestas de La Paz—ten days each May when La Paz celebrates Cortés's disastrous attempt to found it in 1534. La Paz is casual about time, but the Gershwin concert had to be punctual because the Café Chanate shared a plaza where rock bands played every night during the fiesta, and there was no way a piano could compete. Nora had the manager of the sound system drop a mike into the piano and connect it to the outdoor speakers. Eight o'clock was far too early for Paceños and we started with no one in the café, but the tables soon filled with people who had followed the music through the speakers from blocks away. Young rockers hovered at the window by the piano, unexpectedly immersed in the music. After days of being tormented by plug-in guitars, it was sheer joy to retaliate on a creaking upright with the *Rhapsody in Blue*.

Concerns were misplaced that the American-owned Café Chanate would not be patronized by locals, and it even became the site of La Tecla Perpetua's greatest social debacle. I had just participated in Iberê's duo piano concert of short pieces, some involving two players at each piano, for a grand total of nineteen pianists. There were so many guests for the celebration afterward that rather than overwhelm someone's house we invaded the Chanate. We joined the tables in a grand U and sat as if at a banquet. As I ordered my beer, I noticed several carafes of what appeared to be water. Wineglasses were distributed, the carafes were poured, toasts were made, and the clear liquid proved to be tequila. When I had nearly finished my glass, someone tipped it over, apologized, refilled it, and I downed it during the next round of toasts. The seat next to Lupe the socialite was vacant and she gestured for me to join her. She filled the empty wineglass in front of me with tequila. The tequila was her contribution to the evening, she said; it was a special brew that wasn't sold commercially and that her husband obtained from the interior. Wasn't it delicious? I felt compelled to sip and appreciate while Lupe told me she had actually gotten her disco-crazed husband to the concert, though he refused to come backstage afterward and greet her friends. Suddenly the two beers and the three tequilas collided in my brain. I felt socially incapacitated and I slipped away, grateful to have arrived on foot.

I learned next day that the party had lasted three hours after my midnight departure. By that time Lupe had passed out. One of the women took her home, tucked her into a guest bed, then called Lupe's husband to assure him that she was in good hands and would be home in the morning. Rather than thanking the Samaritan and apologizing for any inconvenience, he and Lupe's brother charged over to the house, seized Lupe, told her that she was never again to talk to any members of La Tecla Perpetua, threatened to confiscate her piano and declared the music school off-limits when she wasn't teaching. Furthermore, she would no longer be corrupted by classical music at home, for the house was henceforth to be free of all but the sensible strains of disco and rock. Knowing the men's mindset, said Lupe's friend, if any of the males of the group—Iberê or Fernando or I—had been on the premises, merely having a drink in the parlor while Lupe was sleeping it off, there would have been further hell to pay.

"Lupe's family treats her like a servant," I said to Lupe's friend.

"No," she replied, "people like that already have servants, who are people to the extent that they are useful. When a woman is more lovely and giving than they deserve, she turns into a piece of furniture."

TO USE THE PIANO as a passport to a locale's interior does not always lead to views of joy, but the paths are revelatory and I still hoped that one might lead to "Mata Hari." In 1992, two nights before I left La Paz, I learned that the composer's nephew, Pichu Peláez, was playing piano in an Italian restaurant called Ciao. I listened until his break, then asked if he could play "Mata Hari," by Luis Peláez.

"I don't play it," Pichu calmly replied, "but I do have a tape of it." I implored him for a copy and he promised to bring one the following night. When I returned on the eve of my departure, I was told it was Pichu's night off.

Maddeningly, the music had slipped away one more time. When I returned to La Paz, Ciao had closed and Pichu was spending time on the mainland. Just before I left La Paz in 1993, I learned that Pichu was managing the gallery where Iberê held his duo piano concerts. I showed up with a blank cassette and asked for "Mata Hari." The next day Pichu returned the cassette with the music and told me the circumstance of the recording. Quichu, who had pestered the old composer for his music and also realized it was going to die with him, arranged to meet him one day at the music school and arrived with a tape recorder running in her purse. She asked if he would play his compositions in one of the practice rooms, purely for her enjoyment. He played his trademark "Costa Azul," a march of his devising, then "Mata Hari." I took the tape triumphantly back to Aspen and worked it out in my house.

The piece was still elusive and I realized I was naive to think I could have caught it if the composer had run through it a few more times. He played it three times on the tape. Half of the piece—the part I nearly remembered—remained fixed between playings, but the second half wandered over a loose pattern and was clearly part improvisation. A second reason for his not writing it down might have been that it hadn't quite jelled, even for him—and, furthermore, that indeterminacy was part of the very character of "Mata Hari." In this lone survival of the music, the notes were muffled by the folds of Quichu's purse, with extraneous notes added by a child practicing scales in the next room. Aside from Quichu's exclamation, "¡Qué bonita!" at the conclusion of "Mata Hari," her voice and the composer's are too blurred to decipher. Overheard as if through a series of veils, the music remained as fugitive as the figure who inspired it, and anyone who tried it would have to extemporize. I played it over and over, experimenting with the free part, and came up with my own slightly unstable version of "Mata Hari."

I had the music at last and wanted to make it public, but in 1994 there were no recitals in the offing. That left the Chanate. When Nora asked for an event during the Fiestas de La Paz, I proposed a night of Mexican and La Paz music, with photocopied lyrics so the audience could sing along, all to conclude with the reintroduction of "Mata Hari." Nora got the event listed on the official calendar of events, and I told the story of the music in full during a radio interview two weeks before. Nora set the time with the manager of the sound system. We were to commence at 7:30 sharp, for the first band would begin at nine.

When I arrived at 7:30, the Chanate was empty. No matter, said Nora; they've changed the schedule and we can't have the mike now anyway. Gradually those who came for the event filtered in, including the strong voices I had asked to lead the singing. But the plaza emcee introduced one band after another and wouldn't tell Nora when we could start. By nine, when our program was supposed to be over, those who had come for it had left, including the booming voices. It wasn't until 10:30—three hours after the time listed on the calendar and plugged on the radio—that the host in the plaza announced that a program of Mexican music was about to begin in the Café Chanate. A crowd of total strangers surged in and filled the tables. Nora passed out song lyrics, a mike was dropped in the piano and I plunged in.

Without the strong voices to lead, people sang quietly, but the mood was more of nostalgia than self-consciousness. As I got to the last song, "Costa Azul"—the official state song by Luis Peláez that was to precede "Mata Hari"—I heard another band cranking up in the plaza. The rockers had found a way to shortcut the mike, but I was not going to be stopped from playing "Mata Hari." I stood up and shouted a single sentence in Spanish that I was about to play a lost piece of music called "Mata Hari," by La Paz's own composer, Luis Peláez Manríquez, and played it as loudly as the piece's impressionism would tolerate. When I finished, someone shouted back, "That was beautiful! Would you play it again?" I did. Then the roar from the plaza overcame all and the event was over. When I got over my exasperation at the interference, I realized that "Mata Hari"—sought by my failing memory, pursued in failed appointments, finally caught through the fabric of a purse and against a child's scales—had once more been glimpsed, as was now tradition, behind an updated veil.

The next morning a tiny ill-dressed man came up to me on the street and tapped my arm. Winter carnival and the

Fiestas de La Paz are the only times that the city is afflicted with beggars, and I was prepared to be asked for money. "I just wanted to thank you for the Mexican music last night," he said, "especially that last thing you played, that 'Mata Hari.' That was extraordinary. I hope I can hear it again."

TO BLEND ONE'S CONSCIOUSNESS with the universe seems pretentious to a Westerner and to strive for ego loss seems a contradiction in terms—but I was briefly tricked into something like it one late afternoon, driving through Monument Valley. The stranded formations were deep-shadowed, russet and cayenne in the low sun. A few horses wandered in scrawny solitude and each sage seemed lit an independent silver-green. I was enjoying it all in a touristic way, in that last light that flares each object with its own radiance, and particularly I relished the shadow of my own jeep passing over the sage like an elongated Model T. To be the eccentric eye through all that deepened color was personally satisfying. Suddenly the jeep passed into the shadow of a monument, the image I so identified with vanished, and the rest of my awareness was sprung loose. For an instant I felt, this is how the place would feel without an

Time Out

external intelligence: landscape *aware of itself.* My thought spread out for a moment, freed from its source; then I caught myself being aware of my own absence, identity flooded back, and long before the jeep emerged from shadow my brain was back in my skull.

THE METAPHYSICAL TENT is made of real nylon. It is pitched in clean arroyos, lush meadows, woods on a warm starry night, peaceful streambanks, sandbars and plateaus—anywhere their air is delicious, the stars brilliant and the sounds of darkness busy with a subdued and comforting music. The metaphysical tent is not drawn against weather. It is drawn against snakes, scorpions, tarantulas, kissing bugs, Gila monsters, bears, bats, griffins, pterodactyls, werewolves, voyeurs: all the evil projections and chimeras of the human skull. The metaphysical tent is a sedative, a stiff drink, an all-night station, Mother's nylon arms. It catches the body only by mistake. The body meanwhile suffers sweat, stickiness, musty clothing, jamming of the ear, insomnia, boredom and its own gathering smell. The fearful brain and the captive body cohabit under the meta-

The
Metaphysical
Tent

physical tent until the red-eye of dawn, when the stakes are pulled, the cords folded in, the nylon rolled and crammed into a stuff bag, the stuff bag loaded into a backpack, and the metaphysical tent steals heavily away.

GUERRERO NEGRO, a town I had long treated as a beer-and-gas stop midway down the peninsula, always struck me as small but monotonous. Here the word *salary*, literally "salt money," returned to its roots, for nearly every citizen worked for the world's largest evaporative salt operation or its support businesses. City blocks in unvarying rectangles democratically apportioned the potholes and dust. Pacific fogs broke mid-morning or shrouded the town all day. Interest was briefly sparked by fences made from a yucca called *datilillo*, whose posts had taken root and seasonally sprouted and bloomed—and, while it lasted, the curiously named Bermuda Triangle Billiard Parlor. Salt company officials lived in a small but trim suburban area distanced from ramshackle plebeian housing by a well-tended park; more indicative of the town's status was a Quonset hut post office that retained a permanently transient quality even

Salt on
Their Tales

as the company became a world player in the salt market. An artist from La Paz told me that oxidation from the briny air gave an interestingly rusty cast to the litter. Once, waiting in line for unleaded, I counted an even hundred turkey vultures on the microwave tower over town.

GUERRERO NEGRO blossomed into an unlikely spur to adventure when I chanced to meet a biologist from Mexico City who had moved there to work for the federal interior department. Fernando Heredia had taken a better-paying job with the salt operation but remained a volunteer in a program to protect the peninsular pronghorn, an endangered subspecies of the animal most Americans refer to, inaccurately, as the antelope. I had once seen the Sonoran pronghorn, another endangered subspecies, in the Cabeza Prieta Wildlife Refuge in Arizona, and had been struck by its size, delicacy and speed. The pronghorn was the swiftest sustained runner in the world and had been clocked up to ninety-five kilometers per hour for several minutes at a time. Its eyes were like eight-power binoculars. The Baja California population, which had diverged in isolation, once numbered in the thousands and roamed an area eight hundred kilometers in length, from San Felipe and San Quintín in the north to the latitude of Bahía Magdalena in the south. Despite a risky curiosity, pronghorn don't tolerate much human presence. Hunting and the disruption of habitat had so decimated the population that Mexico made the killing of pronghorns illegal in 1922. A census of the peninsula in 1925, conducted by unknown means, found roughly five hundred animals. When censuses resumed in 1977, the peninsular pronghorn was confined to a single area within the Vizcaíno Desert of the mid-peninsula, a stretch of lowlands projecting into the Pacific between the whale-breeding waters of Scammon's Lagoon and Laguna San Ignacio. Census figures had since hovered around one hundred, dropping in December 1990 to as few as twenty-two animals.

When SEDUE—then the Mexican environmental department's acronym—first undertook to protect the remaining animals, they began with a ploy also popular in the United States, the poisoning of coyotes. Coyotes, and in rare cases mountain lions, did take occasional young, but the three species had long led lives in balance and poisoning was soon seen to be futile. SEDUE then turned its attention to educating ranchers and townspeople, particularly inhabitants in the coastal villages between the two lagoons, who made their living harvesting wildlife of the sea. Signs warned that penalties for shooting pronghorn included fines and up to three years in jail. The peninsular subspecies looked enough like other pronghorn that outside trophy hunters weren't considered a threat, but the small gene pool left the population vulnerable to inbreeding and disease. The best insurance seemed a second, captive population.

Unexpectedly, an opportunity opened up. In 1986, Exportadora de Sal, the salt company, enlarged its complex of evaporation ponds so as to wholly surround an area of former pronghorn habitat fifty thousand hectares in extent, known as La Mesa de la Cholla. The sprawling hill was covered with native vegetation, moated by basins of seawater and an impassable canal, and all points of access were controlled by Exportadora. A few fawns could be captured shortly after birth and transferred to the island, where they could be bottle-fed in an enclosure for three months, then raised on vegetation grown on-site. Predators would be banished, and adult pronghorn could later be introduced so as to have a diverse breeding population. If the captive animals flourished, some could be transferred to the species' current habitat and eventually—once human beings had been persuaded not to shoot them—returned to areas in which they had been exterminated. Experts in animal capture from the United States, the country with the most pronghorns, had been down to investigate, and Mexican biologists had conferred with them in Minnesota. The grand plan would be formulated by the Center for Biological Investigations in La Paz, coordinated by SEDUE, and financed by Exportadora. The first capture was set for February 1991, three months after I heard about it. I asked Fernando, the biologist I had met, whether I could watch if I kept out of the way. I didn't have to stand aside; I could help.

In the three months between Fernando's invitation and the proposed capture, SEDUE reconsidered its resources and knowledge, knew they couldn't afford to jeopardize a single animal and opted for another year of study. Fernando told me I was still welcome to visit the habitat, but when the head of SEDUE in La Paz heard about an expedition he hadn't authorized, he summoned me to his office. After a crisp exchange he allowed me to enter the area with SEDUE officials and conduct an unofficial census if I paid all expenses. I enlisted a friend in La Paz and, unsure what to expect, we arrived in Guerrero Negro on February 28, 1991.

WE CERTAINLY DIDN'T EXPECT that SEDUE's three Guerrero Negro employees—charged with overseeing mid-peninsula resources that included cave paintings, whale-breeding lagoons, and the Vizcaíno Desert with its rare plants and endangered pronghorns—had no vehicle they trusted out of town. Once they had numbered up to nine people, with dependable wheels, but bureaucratic support fluctuated wildly. At the moment they were down to two former Exportadora pickups rusted out from years of driving between salt ponds, and until we arrived they couldn't even get out to where their duties lay. But by a stroke of timing we arrived at sundown on the last day of the month, just when they piled into the pickups to count the town's osprey population in the brief time between the birds' return to the nest and nightfall.

Upon the system of wires that distributed electricity from the diesel generating plant, ospreys had assembled their vast, shaggy nests. Wherever a post formed a corner, sprouted a branch, or supported a couple of crosspieces with insulators, these fish-eating eagles had tossed their salads of sticks and trash. Fernando said that bird electrocutions were rare, but over the years so many damp sticks had been dropped across the wires, shorting the current and blackening parts of town, that enraged citizens once pressured the electric company into dismantling all the nests. To the delight of SEDUE officials, the birds immediately rebuilt. SEDUE talked the electric company into building platforms for nests above its wires and convinced the public that the privilege of hosting ospreys was worth the occasional blackout. Our count turned up thirty-three ospreys, which particularly pleased the officials in that a recent French visitor reported that there were only three nesting pairs in all of France.

Fascinated by the huge nests in the dusk, I revisited them on foot the next morning. The stick piles had been colonized by sparrows that swarmed in and out of their nests within nests, and cries of ospreys that stayed home to raise their young shrilled through Guerrero Negro's clamor of radios and combustion. Fewer than half of the ospreys had taken advantage of the pallets nailed up by the electric company. By osprey standards it seemed more chic to rig the nest on the electrical system and to innovate with burlap and plastic bags. The prize, I decided on my house tour, went to a creation that shaded an oversized tire where women with small children rested while making the social rounds. Engulfing its few sticks were palm fronds, strips of canvas, turquoise fishnet, torn clothing, pieces of rope, a garland of plastic ivy, a hem of blue tarp, blanket shreds, the brush end of a broom, a fan belt, a hanger, pantyhose and shredded Visqueen—an entire airborne landfill—upon which the architect glared at me through the pinhole of his yellow eye as if daring me to dispute his taste.

With a census already under our belts, we bought three days' worth of food, signed the papers that let the two of us from La Paz plus Fernando and a SEDUE official through the gates of Exportadora, and roared off in the jeep toward the salt flats. After years of peering toward the mists of Scammon's Lagoon and reading about the salt harvest, I thought I knew what to expect. I knew the company was 51 percent national and 49 percent owned by Mitsubishi of Japan and that, beginning in 1957, a system of dikes and canals had converted the broad tidal flats of the lagoon into evaporation ponds that now occupied 250 square kilometers. Water entered a gate and made a three-year pilgrimage through thirteen enormous ponds, each more saline than the one before, as seawater evaporated and rendered its salt. Pacific winds and steady noonday sun speeded the process. Each pond was precisely one meter deep, so closely calculated that aside from ten pumps at the entrance and two along the way, the entire system was kept imperceptibly in motion by a tiny drop in elevation. Exportadora boasted that its products were pure and "the only chemicals are wind and sun." Actually the process was not so simple. Seawater contains algae and other organic materials, as well as sulfur and various minerals, and all need to be removed or condensed out. In ponds

4 through 6, microorganisms were introduced to decrease the reflection of light and increase its absorption. Table salt precipitated out first, then salts of magnesium and potassium. Harvesting machines collected 2,000 tons of salt per hour from the last pond and dispatched it to a washing plant, where it was pelted with a brine spray that brought its purity to 99.7 percent. A conveyor loaded the salt onto barges that floated it in elongated pyramids to nearby Isla Cedros. Ships that could stash up to 7,500 tons of salt hauled it to other ports in Mexico, the United States and Asia—coarse-grained for water softeners, deicing and industrial use; fine-grained for table use. Japan, whose national palate is commonly identified with soy sauce, got half its salt from Guerrero Negro.

As we drove onto the dikes between the ponds, my image of saline mechanics was overwhelmed by billowing color and light. The air was dense with moisture, radiant, cool and fishy. Rectangular ponds suggesting snowfields stretched on either side of causeways of packed sand as we skimmed on a single track. Some basins were so mistily blue that only a white line of salt divided water from sky; others were pink with algae or tinged a corrosive green. Because different salinities bred different insects and marine life, certain ponds were favored by curlews or yellow-legged sandpipers or avocets, so that each pond took on different geometric patterns from the forms and markings of its birds. We paused to watch more than two hundred waders making an angular design with the spindly legs that give them their English name, stilt, and the white bellies and black backs that give them the Spanish *monjita*, little nun. Eared grebes skimmed the surface by the hundreds in lines of smoke; northern shovelers and lesser scaups gathered in separate flotillas; flocks of sandpipers turned in flight like filings of a single mind—dark and striped backs that pivoted en masse, nearly disappearing, to re-form as clouds of pale breasts. Certain areas featured a preponderance of white: white pelicans with their black wing tips hidden in folds, great and snowy egrets, blue herons in the white phase, as if they had all been dipped in salt. Marbled godwits suddenly burst from the surface with perfect spacing between each bird, forming an elongated cloud that swelled, shrank and drew itself out like a single sky serpent in a shifting lens. Some rectangles of water were so wide, their horizons so low, that they seemed the sea itself, and their spume blew onto our tracks like meringue. Occasionally we were jolted by having to make room for yellow trucks whose tires were as big as our jeep and whose gondolas were blinding with salt. Over subsequent censuses this skimming of the salt ponds became my favorite driving anywhere, and Fernando remarked that he had a colleague who drove the thirty kilometers of causeways for sport, attaining non-bird-watching speeds of up to 120 kilometers per hour.

The last causeway ushered us onto La Mesa de la Cholla. After the evaporation ponds, this imagined haven for baby pronghorns was spectacularly nondescript, a wide elevation of scrubby plants. At its far end ten small yellow pumps straddled seawater, initiating its three-year drifting separation toward commerce and sky.

Seabirds, human geometry and screaming pumps dropped behind when we crossed the canal, and the silent dunes that ring Scammon's Lagoon received us with the earthy, medicinal smell of a weed called *manzanilla de coyote*. We had arrived at the bleakest, westernmost extension of the Vizcaíno Desert. The strange trees and endemic plants for which the Vizcaíno is known faded here to isolated shrubs and low vegetation. It was hard to believe that the pronghorns could get all the moisture they needed from these leathery leaves and the dew on their surface, but with no open water in their habitat, these greens were their drink as well as their food. There was no mistaking the plants' toughness, visible in the way their talonlike roots built cones of sand that held in the wind. Normally such shrubs provided a mere dusting of green over gritty sand, but 1991 was gloriously abnormal. Recent rains had broken six years of drought, and wildflowers awaiting this grace had burst into stabs and sweeps of color. Horned larks darted and swooped from our wheels as we followed, lost, and refound tracks made by Pemex, the national oil company, which prospected here in the 1970s; found three wells of natural gas; capped them without revealing which of their many wells they were; and had so far held them in reserve. It was these roads, ruled in straight lines over the pitch of terrain and now nearly lost in vegetation and blowing sand, that we frequently took in search of pronghorns.

We shifted into four-wheel and crawled several kilometers down a rocky arroyo. Abandoning the car, we climbed a rust-colored hill where "you can always see pronghorns." We scanned the circumference for the animals' white rump patches, fur they can actually flare outward, using special muscles, to signal danger to one another. Fernando set up the SEDUE telescope. Through the grainy enlargement it was possible to make out a moving Pleiades that melted as soon as it wobbled into focus. We walked for an hour toward the far specks. The pronghorn vanished, but as we trudged back to the car against the sun, my eyes, driven downward, were dazzled by small yellow flowers called *airito*, or little airs; blue starbursts of wild onion; and magenta clouds of sand verbena, called *alfombrilla*, or little rugs.

We drove back up the arroyo, mashed flowered-over tracks until dark and camped for the night. Distant rains lingered, and under a full moon we could see a downpour in the mountains to the east. Clouds circled the horizon, climbed a third of the way into the sky and hemmed us like a broken bowl. Suddenly Fernando exclaimed and pointed opposite the moon, where an arc of rain and moonlight stood unbroken. It was a moonlit rainbow. I had seen the effect once before, more dimly, in Nevada, but hadn't otherwise heard or read about it and didn't know its name. Binoculars vaporized rather than focused it, but to the naked eye it appeared to shade from orange above to green within. As we sat for more than an hour watching the phenomenon, I asked what distinguished the peninsular pronghorn from other subspecies. Fernando said that the differences in markings were slight, the most significant being a darker coloration. The important variation was behavioral, a life cycle that diverged several months from that of other subspecies, with mating in June and July instead of September and October, and parturition in late January and early February instead of April to June. Because this displaced biological clock had evolved on the peninsula, it was unlikely that another subspecies could be introduced into Baja California and survive. It would be the peninsular pronghorn or none.

As we broke camp in the morning, a truck with three ranchers pulled up. Had we seen any cattle? No, said Fernando; had they seen any pronghorns? Adding up sightings, they had recently seen twenty-three, assuming no animals were counted twice. When they left, I asked Fernando whether cows didn't compete with pronghorns for precious forage. "Ranchers claim that cows and pronghorns eat the same thing during wet years when there's plenty of vegetation, like now, but during drought they specialize in different plants."

"Isn't that just the kind of answer you'd expect from ranchers?" I asked.

"Sure, but we don't have to take their word for it. A biologist in La Paz is studying the impact of cattle. We should know soon."

We had driven no more than a half hour beyond our campsite when Fernando spotted a pair of sticks pointing from a far bush. We bailed out, confirmed them as horns through binoculars, then moved noiselessly forward as they stayed put. I was suddenly aware that the others were drably dressed while I was flagrant in a red sweatshirt, but it was too late to change. After we had covered half the distance we began to walk with deeply bent knees to obscure ourselves, remaining upright to keep track of the horned bush, advancing in the Groucho Marx slide until my back cried for relief. We stopped behind a bush of our own, and through the binoculars I could see the spurs on the front of the horns that give the pronghorn its name. We also spotted a female behind the bush and two recently born pronghorns sprawling in the foliage in front of it. A newborn sprang to its feet and collapsed back in the weeds. "Do you have anything red?" whispered Fernando. I laughed and indicated my whole sweatshirt. "Are you wearing an undershirt?" he asked, apparently concerned for my warmth. I peeled to it and handed him the sweatshirt. "Pronghorns are attracted to red," he whispered, flipping the shirt on top of our bush and prodding it with a stick. There was no reaction from the other bush.

Fernando handed me my sweatshirt on the end of his stick, then advanced on all fours. I tied the red sleeves around my neck and crawled behind him. We stopped at another bush, twice as close as the previous one. Fernando took my shirt again and poked it provocatively on top of the bush. A mockingbird chattered like an informant on a tree behind us. The female pronghorn stepped from behind her bush and peered with interest. Hesitantly she made her way forward, starting, stopping, as if conscious that curiosity was mastering sense. She halted some twenty-five meters away, stared a moment, then retreated to her bush. The male then took his turn, ambling steadily until he was huge to the naked eye, fully detailed through binoculars.

I had never been so close to any variety of pronghorn and was struck by the long, firm jaw. The horns especially had an assertive flourish, thrusting forward with the prongs, then curling back at the tip. The fur of this darker subspecies shone burnished cinnamon in the sun. Most winning up close were the eyes—huge, dark and moist, with long, upwardly turned lashes one would term, by human standards, glamorous. After both sides had satisfied their mutual curiosity, the family of four took off with a delicate bounce.

Relieved of our crouch, we went to see what they had been eating. Their bush, *frutilla*, is known to be pronghorn forage, but they had been cropping flowers. Tracks swarmed all over, the adults' the length of my thumb, the fawns' a bit larger than my thumbnail, angled forward in the form of two-chambered hearts. I reminded Fernando that he had told me the male takes off after birth, leaving the young to be tended by the female. "This was an exception," he explained.

Over the next day and a half we spotted many more pronghorns, none so close as the shirt inspectors, but occasionally in larger groups. We worked toward the Pacific, scanning the flats with binoculars, setting up the scope, trying to fix for each other where a group of white dots stood out from the fawn-colored earth by aligning them with distant peaks of the Sierra Santa Clara, or mid-distance brush and cactus. The distinguishing white of the pronghorns' backs winked on and off like lighthouses. We also saw, singly, four coyotes, all fat and healthy—from gulping a wet year's bounty of rodents, we hoped, not baby pronghorns. At a crossroads near the Pacific, by a road to the fishing villages, we came upon a SEDUE sign warning of fines and jail terms for killing pronghorns.

Unexpectedly we ran into three men sinking a new well. We peered into the hole: surrounded by cement and doubled by a reflection at the bottom, it looked far deeper than its three meters. No, they informed us, they had not struck water, they had merely poured in enough to soften the earth and make digging easier. They lowered themselves to the bottom by rope, loosened the earth with a pick and hauled it up in a bucket. The actual water table, they figured, was at least double that depth.

Was this a new ranch? I asked as we left. No, said the SEDUE official with us, it was part of the *ejido*, the communal farm that ran cattle and owned a vast part of the desert through which we had passed. The three men were professional well diggers the ejido had hired, and as men in an unfamiliar location, far from a source of food, they were just the sort to pick off a pronghorn.

"Does the ejido have permission to put in the well?" I asked.

"Not from us," said the SEDUE official, "and we'll be looking into it. But they need three permissions in all, one from us, one from Recursos Hidráulicos, which manages the water, and one from the county government in Santa Rosalía. Any one of them can deny permission."

"And if the agencies disagree about the well, who wins?"

"You mustn't think of this system as a hierarchy, with one agency over another. They are all separate."

"So if there is a disagreement among agencies, the matter winds up in court?"

"That's the American system. We don't have courts that decide such matters. We appeal to higher authorities, and the party with the most pull wins. The ejido, for instance, is politically powerful and might appeal to the governor's office, or the governor himself, even though SEDUE denied permission to put in the well. Ejidos are older and have more pull than SEDUE. I personally doubt whether this well is going to strike water, but just by being here people drive away the pronghorns and the habitat shrinks. That's why the captive breeding program is so important."

By the end of three days, our unofficial census, which covered most of the known habitat, had found sixty-seven animals. I also had glimpsed the human complication that protecting pronghorns could breed.

THE DRAMATIC LIVE CAPTURE that first lured me to the pronghorn program was further postponed, pending more censuses and study, but having seen the creature in its habitat I became a chronic volunteer. SEDUE had lost the aerial support that had once helped with the census, and I recruited a friend who piloted for Project LightHawk, an American nonprofit that flew light planes for environmental projects. The pilot arrived in February 1992, with only two available days. We were unable to muster a ground crew to coordinate with him, and two SEDUE officials and I joined him in the four-seater, flying transects at one hundred feet over likely terrain.

Having learned the area through immersion, I was curious to see how it was laid out. Salt ponds almost wholly encrusted bladder-shaped Scammon's Lagoon. Currents of the bay, driven by seven-foot tides, made pinwheels of turquoise, aquamarine and cobalt through which gray whales—enormous even from the air—swam in pairs, single file, at random. The collage of light and dark splotches on their skin, caused by barnacles and amphipods that colonize them from birth, showed even more strikingly than from a boat. As we droned to and from the Viz-caíno Desert, I realized that whalewatching by plane would be still more intrusive than by skiff, even as I tasted its forbidden clarity. And we saw, alas, more whales than pronghorns, for our hours of transects roused only twelve animals. We trusted they were beyond the confines of our search rather than wiped out, and the pilot remarked how strong and vibrant were the few we spotted compared with the ratty specimens he had flown over in Wyoming. I noted how the wide grid of one-lane tracks put in by Pemex in the seventies, at times nearly invisible on the ground, was still clear from the sky. The SEDUE officials noted how fresh ranching activity had generated new, up-graded roads that were exerting more human pressure.

NOW THAT I had participated in censuses by land and by air, I was eager to experience the modes in combination. SEDUE and the Center for Biological Investigation in La Paz made plans to count the animals three times a year—in April, to doc-ument the newborns; in June, to see how many young had sur-vived the first months; and in early December, when the animals gathered in herds and were most easily counted. If the prong-horns consistently numbered more than one hundred, the cap-ture could be reconsidered. Meanwhile, the very fact of our being seen in the field five days at a time, with a plane over-head, strengthened the notion that people who bothered the animals might wind up in jail.

Another LightHawk pilot volunteered for the next census, then the job was taken over on a regular basis by Sandy Lanham, a woman from Tucson who ran a one-person environmental aviation program specializing in Mexico. In theory, the plane was to spot the animals, the ground forces were to verify the sightings and each was to advise the other on where to look. In practice, radio contact consistently broke down. We could communicate only when the plane was nearly overhead, and whatever ground radio we mustered for a given census faithfully crackled dead by the third morning. Such censuses must have looked strange to their rare witnesses. Once, we arrived at a new illegal ranch at the end of a suspiciously traveled spur. As we grilled the inhabitants and learned that they had been sent there by a cooperative in Bahía Tortugas, the plane appeared after a two-day absence. I whipped out the radio and, as the plane circled our party, screamed in two languages into its tiny microphone. The plane sped off, one of our officials informed the ranchers that the cooperative would be receiving an official complaint about their ranch, and we roared away in a government pickup and a jeep with Colorado plates. As soon as we had left, our second pickup showed up looking for us, and on learning which way we went, took off in pursuit. As the dust settled, I wondered what the ranchers, who claimed to know nothing of endangered pronghorns, made of such madness. The result of this scrambled procedure was two simultaneous surveys, one from the air and one from the ground. Combining them was possible only because, for the duration of the census, the pronghorns generally maintained their groupings—say, one male, three females and one newborn—and by eliminating similar groups we calculated the population.

Unforeseen was the degree to which endangered pronghorns pursued me to La Paz. I had befriended a biologist who was studying pronghorn habits, nutrition and the impact of cows, and who was the leading proponent of the live capture. He represented the Center for Biological Investigations in La Paz. His opposite number at SEDUE, a biologist turned bureaucrat, felt that the capture was dangerous and that the animals

were better off dying of natural causes than by human interference. Both sides had defensible positions, analogous to a recent debate about whether the last California condors should
be left in the wild or bred in captivity. The underlying problem was that the two men despised each other personally and
refused to communicate. Their institutions were locked into the
program as partners, but the bureaucrat convened meetings
without the biologist and the biologist wouldn't telephone the
bureaucrat. I went back and forth with messages and positions,
and finally took the biologist in person to SEDUE headquarters and explained his position for him to the bureaucrat. When
the bureaucrat suddenly committed to all the support we requested, I felt that my own role in the program had eerily
switched from jeep driver to shuttle diplomat and facilitator.

Prickliness and animosities even followed us to the eve of
departure in Guerrero Negro, where a biologist once complained that SEDUE officials had unfairly pulled rank on him
over seats in the aerial census and that the salt company hadn't
bought enough food for the ground contingent. When I replied
that there were numerous boxes of food, that this wasn't the
moment for perfectionism and it was time to count pronghorns,
he countered that perfectionism was obligatory when dealing
with endangered animals and he boarded the bus back to La Paz
before we started. Just as communications were improving in
La Paz, the difficult bureaucrat quit because his programs
weren't being funded, President Salinas reorganized SEDUE
itself—replacing higher officials and changing its acronym to
SEDESOL—and a new bureaucrat had to be educated about
the pronghorn program. The newcomer asked me if I realized that La Mesa de la Cholla, the intended refuge for baby
pronghorns, had only one of the three vegetational types that
pronghorns eat in their yearly cycle. The biologist studying

pronghorn forage told me he had never heard of such a fact and why was I, a nonbiologist volunteer, even being asked such a question? At that point I realized that I would rather help pronghorns in the desert than in La Paz, and I withdrew from the fray.

Mercifully, once we pulled through the Exportadora gates and headed toward the pronghorn counts, tensions dropped away and all worked professionally together. The itinerary became familiar: across the salt basins to the dunes, through the arroyos, over the inland flats and mesas, south to the coast, then out five days later on bone-rattling washboard, completing a grand loop. In the absence of rain, tiny plants made a ratty carpet between freestanding tangles of barbs. The expanses were silent, with often no sound but the wheeze of a gnatcatcher or the gurgling of a black-throated sparrow until we turned our ignitions. On side trips when we didn't need my jeep, I sat on a drum of gas in the back of a pickup and watched the mottled desert floor with its sweeps of *vidrillo*, a plant as rusty as the cinders it thrives on. The first couple of days we were routinely alarmed at the scarcity of pronghorns, and the first sightings were always an event. On one nervous count we climbed out of an arroyo and caught our first pronghorn in a mound of greenery, then another and another until a group of seven had opened like a fan. On the next count we saw only loners until the third day, when we drove up a mesa behind our camp. There, to our disbelief, were herds—thirteen here, twenty-four over there—tearing across the brush radiant with well-being.

Censuses took character from changing personnel. Besides being joined by rotating government officials, we were once accompanied by a biologist who came to study burrowing owls. Along the clay banks of the arroyos lay small holes with dripping white entrances, and occasionally a small pale face that withdrew as we approached. While a SEDUE official carped at this deviation from our mission, the biologist gathered regurgitated pellets and wrapped them in foil for later analysis. On a far different census, four SEDUE officials were replaced at the last minute by four workers from Exportadora. They had no knowledge of pronghorns and did not even possess binoculars, but their truck was well stocked and their leader was an excellent chef.

Also distinguishing various trips were inevitable car problems. The rusted trucks that couldn't leave town in 1991 were patched and back in the field two years later, but at the beginning of that census I had to haul both out of the dunes. Many of the flat tires were caused by the tough needles of the frutilla, and I realized that in addition to providing food and cover, this ally of the pronghorn also stabbed the wheels of their main predator. On the trip with the salt workers, my jeep mysteriously stopped. One found that the carbon had fallen out of the distributor so that it didn't pass current and announced that we needed to find the old kind of flashlight battery with a carbon core. Another almost instantly picked one out of the sand, cut out the core, popped a piece of it into the distributor, and in five minutes we were off. Everywhere we camped for the duration of that trip, the salt workers found and clipped old batteries until I amassed an envelope full of carbon. Their improvisations weren't confined to mechanics, for when we camped in a spot with no firewood because their truck had two flats at once, they stuck two dead yuccas in an abandoned tire and torched it. We gathered around a glow that was steady and pleasant if you didn't get downwind.

Driving back to La Paz—once with the original piece of flashlight battery still passing current at eighty kilometers per hour—I would savor the census's oddities. One April the

Vizcaíno was alive with thousands of migrating monarch but-
terflies glistening orange in the air and splashing yellow on
the windshield. In an empty valley I spotted a surreal burst of
color that resolved through binoculars into a bouquet of lilac
and cream party balloons, from who knows what far birthday,
that had snagged on a frutilla without puncturing. Somewhat
later, a larger cream-colored globe on a similar bush turned
out to be a ferruginous hawk. There was the woman in the
coastal village whose husband had been struck at by a rattler.
The snake had missed his skin, but the woman was so traumatized by the fang holes when she washed his pants that
she no longer ventured outdoors during the hot half of the year.
Most satisfyingly, we ventured beyond pronghorn habitat to
the scavenger beach of Malarrimo, where objects carried by
the California Current from the north are snagged by a spur
that protrudes into the Pacific. We allowed ourselves fifteen
minutes to look for objects other than pronghorns at this
Lourdes of debris. I found an empty flask of mink oil from the
Pacific Cruise Line, a KFC bucket hundreds of miles from
the nearest franchise and a serviceable mauve plastic hanger,
which I kept. As government agents we reminded a handful of
campers not to litter and, surprisingly, were not laughed at on
this beach treasured for its trash. We arrived at the April 1994
census to find that one of the Guerrero Negro biologists had
festooned SEDUE headquarters' mango trees with red bows
so the fruit wouldn't be rotted by an upcoming annular eclipse.
The week before, four pronghorns had been seen parading
past the Guerrero Negro shooting range. Perhaps this was not
an animal we could help . . .

The greatest anomaly was that the live capture, reportedly
three months off when I first heard about it, seemed to recede
as we labored toward it. The biologist who most favored it was

encouraged when the November 1993 census turned up a record 175 animals, then disheartened that the subsequent April count was down to 45. We attributed these fluctuations to our inability at times to find the animals rather than to population bursts and die-offs, but radio-collaring the animals to track their movements would entail the same risks as live capture. Another biologist, equally knowledgeable and serious about the program, opposed the capture because he didn't trust the salt company not to abandon the animals once they were on La Mesa de la Cholla. He pointed out that the whole mid-peninsula was, on paper, a biological reserve in which firearms were illegal, but nobody did anything about it. Given the authority, he would disarm the populace, put wardens in the field, enforce the penalties and leave the pronghorns right where they were. I began to see La Mesa de la Cholla—biologists' dream, bureaucratic concoction, secret garden for baby pronghorns—receding like a mythic golden age rather than advancing like salvation.

Thinking of Guerrero Negro itself, I saw radiating species: ospreys in the center, embraced by salt ponds with their spectrum of seabirds, followed by Scammon's Lagoon with its whales, then the Vizcaíno Desert with its scrub and its pronghorns. One February I was alarmed for the center when I read in a La Paz paper that hurricane-force winds had battered Guerrero Negro. I called Fernando Heredia, the salt company biologist, to learn the consequences. The blast had knocked over his satellite dish, the principal relief from life by the salt ponds. More ominously, osprey nests had been swept to the ground, killing at least one mature osprey and chick, full damage unknown.

When I next arrived in Guerrero Negro, I was relieved to see so much rubbish still poised on the electrical system, and I learned that only three nests had failed to hang tight. I sped to my favorite. Most of its sticks had blown away, leaving pure trash. As I admired a newly revealed paintbrush, a huge form glided into sight. There was a shriek from the nest, a small head craned from the fan belts and pantyhose, and fish fresh from the brine passed from parent to child in sheer defiance against the sky.

TRAVELERS BACK FROM THE WILDERNESS may remark that their trip "passed like a dream" and—as if it were a good night's sleep—that they "hope it lasts." Such phrases may be tossed off without thought of the literal content, but offhand remarks often carry freights of meaning not consciously intended by their speakers, and folk expressions wouldn't have gained currency without a certain resonance. Wilderness addicts are often accused of emotionalism and irrationality. It may be that instead of denying it they should look to their very unreason as a source of strength—and that they ought to ask themselves, in particular, why their experience of the wilds so often invokes the language of sleep.

One's state in the wilderness is anything but drowsy. The very fundamentals—cooking, finding water, getting through the night, keeping warm or cool, staying safe—cannot be taken

Wilderness
and the
Buried Self

for granted. Traveling with a life-support system on one's back and uncertain terrain underfoot, the hiker must watch where to step, keep the load adjusted and arrive at a reasonable camp-site by nightfall. Weather, so easily corrected by a thermostat back home, constantly intrudes with heat, rain, cold, wind, even snow, thunderstorms and flash floods. In tight situations the very basics can compete for attention, requiring a multiplicity of focus otherwise demanded only in fast traffic. Few moments in the wilderness are allowed to pass unnoticed, and it is no wonder that a week in the woods, enjoyed or endured, seems equivalent to three or four weeks at home.

But urbanites do not seek out wilderness to stretch time or complicate the basics; they go to immerse themselves in another context. The more our lands are surfeited by our pres-ence, the more the forces that spawned us retreat from sight. As landscape without our image recedes, the wilds only deepen in their strangeness. Many, of course, have so adapted to mech-anized surroundings that they view the elimination of nature with perfect indifference, as if it didn't involve them, or as if concern for the wilds were a comic aberration. But even those whose alienation from nature produces a hunger for it, deep-ening its allure, find that evolving civilization has given new meanings to nature itself, increasing its psychic remoteness.

The more we clear forests, for instance, the more the re-maining ones surround us with sounds we no longer recognize, coming from mysterious densities. Mountain vistas, traditional sources of inspiration, take on extraterrestrial connotations in this dawn of space exploration. The serpentine webs of canyons, with their water-smoothed knobs, recesses and clefts, may sug-gest some Freudian underworld. Shifts of climate and terrain add unaccustomed turnings of the irrational. The very unfold-ing of a trip—across streams, through valleys, over passes—

assumes aspects of a fable. Backpackers file through noncivilized country more exiled than their forebears, open to increasing dislocation. Their mental state is alert and receptive, with the ego largely in abeyance. The self may assert itself in relation to other campers, but gives way in the face of the nonhuman. That waking trance, in which one is lifted out of oneself and included in something larger, was extolled in the last century as Transcendence. Its very existence—so inconvenient to those with more lucrative plans for the wilds—has been denied by exploiters and developers. But for many the sensation remains a crucial part of their lives, and is known in current jargon as the Wilderness Experience.

Sleep itself, after the buffetings of fresh air, exercise, unaccustomed sights and relief from social pressures, resembles a blackout. Only a novice is tortured by roots and rocks that erupt under bedrolls, or by snapping twigs pregnant with snakes and bears. Anyone who has spent a few nights out without getting killed, or gets tired enough, simply lets go. Those used to a good sleep in the wilds may eventually find their home mattress somehow ungiving after the undulations of bedrock, sand or soft soil.

No one has discovered for certain why most of us vertebrates need to sleep at all, though theories abound. By the use of electroencephalographs that monitor the brain waves of sleepers, we do know that the most restorative sleep alternates between periods of dreaming and periods of mental blankness. There is the sleep when we are participants in irrational fantasies, known as REM sleep for the rapid eye movement that accompanies it, and intervals when the brain takes a complete break. A camping trip—composed of days when life is vivid, unfamiliar and ego-diminished, and nights of sheer oblivion—extends that pattern over a period of days or weeks. Hallucination, blackout; hallucination, blackout: a wilderness trip extends the night's cycle to embrace the waking hours. It is at least teasing that campers back from a satisfying trip feel restored as if after sleep, on a grander scale. And they recall it in sleep's vocabulary.

One recent theory on the function of dreams, expressed by Carl Sagan in *The Dragons of Eden*, is that they give necessary expression to more primitive parts of our brains, developed when we were simpler forms of mammals, and reptiles before that. Our huge neocortex, whose cleverness and adaptability so distinguishes us from other animals, developed rapidly and has had little time to integrate itself with older parts of our psyche. Kept in check during the day by our dominant human consciousness, the instinctive parts of our brain need their own moments of expression, lest they erupt at the wrong time and drive us mad. Dreaming is thus a safety vent for impulses that no longer apply.

If Sagan is right, it may be that the urge to invade the wilds, where one can escape social pressure and wield a more intuitive kind of intelligence, is also related to the need to give expression to older parts of our psyche—a time, perhaps, when we were precivilized hunters, if not earlier mammals and reptiles. The wilderness ambushes us with sights and sensations that demand a quicker, keener kind of response. Abilities we didn't know we had come suddenly into play. The civilized person who meets a primitive demand, instead of feeling demeaned, may experience an unexpected elation. The greater the adventure, the more refreshed the camper is likely to feel afterward. A good camping trip and a dream-filled sleep, in quite different ways, both feel like acts of integration, connecting us with otherwise exiled parts of ourselves.

The human mind is perhaps more tangled than any wilderness we are trying to save, and has connections we are only beginning to make out. It may be that dreaming and wilderness travel are so invigorating because they form bridges to a past still within us, stranded in inaccessible parts of our being. That might explain why a journey to the wilds, with all its elements of chance, discomfort and strangeness, seems for so many like a homecoming, a return to something lost. It might also explain the alleged irrationality of wilderness defenders—and suggest why the need for wilderness, passionately felt, is so hard to articulate, and so crucial to our balance.

SOME OF US DO NOT MOVE very rapidly along the main channel. It is not that our packs are heavy, that we are lazy, that we cannot find our footing, that we cannot decide whether to take the meanders midstream or to shave the corners through the weeds. It is that every few bends there is a breach in the walls, luring us into a darker world which must also be explored.

It is their seduction that a series of side canyons through the same formation are no more alike than we, of standard human flesh, who explore them. I recently spent ten days hiking twenty river miles with fellow canyoneers. By linear standards we were practically at rest, yet we were constantly in motion because of poking into every slot we came to. The first was little more than a recessed seep, ringed by a stand of eight-foot poison ivy red as dried chiles, beneath which a tarantula posed on a rock while I snapped its portrait. The next was one of those dream sagas

Sidewinders
Anonymous

that began like a great cathedral, snaked for three miles the width of a hotel corridor, gave way to banks of cottonwoods by a running stream, then opened to a gallery of towering formations—which might lead onto the encompassing plateau, or might turn you back after fifteen despairing miles. The third dead-ended after five turns beneath a vaulting double arch, animated by a single bat that circled and circled a dark pool so slowly a close-up caught its tiny face. The next canyon was so choked with reeds, grasses, watercress, box elders, scrub oak, nettles and stagnant murk one never quite knew what one was stepping on, nor saw what birds cried from the trees. At the next indentation we merely intended to get out of the heat and found a rattlesnake curled around a limb at eye level, its head nestled peacefully among its soft loops, asleep in the same cool we had sought. Another seeming dead end continued in a slot so fine we proceeded sideways, spelunking and blind, groping our way to the last shaft. The next was a chasm of rubble. The next . . .

Side canyons, even more than their connecting river, give you a sense of something you can't quite name that leads you on. Smells are musky and herbal, or dry and powdery, touched here with an obscure honeysuckle, there with a whiff like clothes steeped in tobacco smoke. Their very obstacles urge you forward. You will fling off your clothes to get through a cold pool, only to chimney above it with a foothold here, an ass-wedge there, up to the next impediment. Faced with an intractable slot, you will backtrack to the last rockslide, scramble up, then proceed along a high shelf until the canyon rises to meet you. You will shinny up a tree, a rotten ledge, a friend's flesh: anything rather than turn back. Most fiendishly, side canyons have side canyons, which in turn sprout side canyons, and if you have squandered a certain amount of energy in the system already, the urge to completeness takes over. You have to see it all, at whatever cost. You find yourself grabbing precarious knobs, working dubious slots, for the madness of one more bend. The addict will stop at nothing, will risk his living flesh to see which way dumb stone will twist next. The end may be one more wall. Or it may be a glimpse of the mountain lion which has eluded you all your life.

Side canyons almost generate their own laws. Shortly after hearing that owls are considered evil omens, I hiked with a friend in a side canyon of the Escalante River and spotted a large owl asleep in shadow over our heads. We were silent for several minutes, hoping he might step forward into sunlight where we could get a better look, and at last my friend tossed a stick against the rock beneath him, to startle him awake. The owl burst out with a great flapping of wings while my camera clicked on blurred stone.

Shortly beyond, the canyon forked. It was getting late, time to turn back, and a boulder the size of a garage stood at the confluence, promising a clear view either way. While my friend waited I scrambled up some rocks, leapt onto the boulder and suddenly felt dizzy. I stood still for a moment, waiting for my head to clear, while everything continued in motion. With a shock I realized the entire rock was unsettled by my weight and was about to topple. I quickly backed off the way I came and regained solid ground. Dizziness gave way to a pounding heart. Out in the mainstream I would never find a connection between a disturbed owl and a treacherous rock. But in a side canyon . . .

The addict knows that to enter a side canyon is to spin the wheel of fortune. His career is a series of tangents, out and back, out and back; like the sidewinder he advances laterally. It does no good to tell him his behavior is about as reasonable as a frayed rope, that his days are a compendium of minutiae, that he cannot see the river for its tributaries. It is useless to appeal to his personal safety. Every unexplored slot is a road not taken, a crossroads ignored, an adventure missed. He is Theseus in the labyrinth, Orpheus in Hades, Uncle Wiggily in search of his fortune, advancing toward he knows not what grail. If his main-channel friends tell him he will never get there, he may reply, with his headful of dead ends, that there is destination in every step.

AMATEUR PIANISTS, obsessive as a breed, are impossible about their hands. When the temperature drops below forty, I conjure frostbite, and recall too often that time I rammed a scorpion with a thesaurus in a Phoenix kitchen and bent my little finger the wrong way. There are moments when the desert, my other obsession, seems to aim every dagger at my clumsy, aspiring technique. And the desert, true to character, landed its blow when I was least on guard.

A friend had stopped to rinse a gravel-choked sneaker in a small pool. I sluffed my pack against a tree and settled on the only perch, a pointed knob of sandstone. I leaned back on one hand to take the rest of my weight, watched my friend dutifully rinse the sock, turn it right side out, wring it, pull it on, cram a wet foot into a wet sneaker, pull the lace, form the bow . . . Suddenly the rock sheared in the middle, and eight

Slickrock and
the Bach Chaconne

inches of sandstone, capped with my bulk, landed on the fourth digit of my right hand.

The nail was instantly black. A bit of blood jetted from the tip, and skin was scraped from the second joint. I felt for broken bones, detected none, and found the rest of my hand unscathed. The finger was less painful than icy and numb; I held it like a cracked fetish as we rushed back up the canyon to camp. There was no remedy but to wash it thoroughly, wrap a Band-Aid around the fingertip and take a belt of 151 proof for perspective.

Because the injury was to my right hand rather than my left, the incident oddly meshed with a more blissful event on a previous canyon trip. Our party included a concert violinist from New York who needed to keep in practice for an upcoming recital. Lashed to his pack was a fiddle whose maker had told him, "It's one of my rejects. Take it to the desert, tell me what it does, and don't worry." Daily we heard a warm-up of scales and figures coming from his hiding place. On the night of the full moon we gathered on a sandstone shelf, someone produced a candle mantled into a manhattan glass, and our friend unfurled the Bach Chaconne. The only other sound was the slur of moving water.

Cold light emptied into the canyon, turning one wall a luminous pocked silver, leaving the other a hulking darkness stopped by a line that inched toward us as the music progressed. I had heard the Chaconne before, with half-attention and most often in orchestral arrangements, and felt I was hearing another piece. As the violin worked through the minor variations, the listeners emerged one by one in the moonlight. We were covered with radiance by the time the music broke into the major. When the piece returned to the dark opening chords, it was impossible not to be struck by the vastness of the architecture, laboring intensely toward peace and celebration, and back to severity. Almost all organized sound seems to profane the desert, or any great landscape. But the Chaconne, with its massive journey from austerity to tenderness and back—as if through rock and water—seemed to concur in shape with the very walls that echoed its passage.

The Chaconne is the last movement of Bach's Partita No. 2 in D minor for violin unaccompanied; it opens from a complete partita like the tail of a peacock and has lived the career of a free-floating monument. Among the transcriptions for assorted instruments is one for piano by Busoni, with two recordings currently in catalog, and a more obscure arrangement by Brahms for the left hand alone. Contrived in 1879 as an exercise to develop the dexterity of the left hand, or perhaps as a musical folly, it sat at the back of my *Brahms Klavier-Werke, Band II*, as a kind of consolation prize if my right hand was ever knocked out of commission. It was, ironically, a canyon in Utah that first revealed to me the immensity of the Bach Chaconne, and a canyon three drainages away that sent me in desperation to the score.

On previous occasions I had lost toenails, watched them grow back in a month, and assumed I had a month to get a grip on the Chaconne. I kept the loose fingernail of the right hand bandaged, lest I snag it off before the replacement was ready, and plugged away at Bach-Brahms. As the new nail took shape in the dark, the opening variations, more pocked than luminous, grew under the strengthening left hand. Take the bandage off and let it breathe, said a medically knowledgeable friend. When the bandage did slip off in the shower, there was my dead nail, now ghostly white, arched over something mysterious. The skin around it was unattractive; better to keep the whole thing under wraps until the job was done. I worked my way to the lush, delicious major. The old nail was looser; I peeked through the end and glimpsed a kind of gray mush. So one hand was semicomposing, the other decomposing . . . I reached the return of the minor. The old nail was half a flange but I didn't dare pry it too far, even for inspection. It was three months since I had sat on the defective rock, and the Chaconne was shakily memorized. For God's sake, let your skin breathe! insisted my knowledgeable friend. When the bandage slid off in the next shower, it took the nail with it. Revealed was the lower half of a new fingernail, looking normal, while the rest was a kind of puckered thickening I was afraid even to touch.

"Is this *normal* for a new fingernail?" I asked my friend. "After all these months, is this all I get?"

"Normal for a pianist. You'd probably have trouble growing toenails if you were a dancer. Look, nails are an evolutionary vestige. They're claws on the way out. If it doesn't grow back all the way, you'll get tough skin that will do just as well."

In another month my right fourth finger sported a smooth, polished nail, indistinguishable from the rest. The Chaconne too was smooth, needing the deepening only time can provide, and meanwhile my left hand, as Brahms intended, was a newly adequate partner to my right. The canyons that led on the one hand to a new nail, and on the other hand to Bach, took millennia to cut to the present depth—but the geological span is a luxury we lack. Time is uneven, unfair, and lands unpredictable blows. It is also the only medium. Whether we're canyons or musicians, we must dig into it and shape what we can.

AS PAVEMENT CLIMBS FROM PHOENIX, the expanse of cactus fractures like a shook jigsaw. Smooth desert suddenly rears into domes, palisades, crenellations and rockfalls, labyrinthine, crazed, a troll's nightmare. The phenomenon is known as exfoliation—literally, the losing of leaves. The substance is granite that cracks at roughly right angles. Once it has been cubed, the corners crumble faster than the faces, a geological way of rounding the square. What the square loses on the way to circlehood is what becomes desert sand. Solid granite? The desert's mother lode is sheer rot, rock on its way to becoming a million square miles of kitty litter.

The whole formation registers a bare mile on the odometer, two drainages splintered by assorted cracked ribs. I had driven through once too often, and one January afternoon, on

Transition Zone

a whim, I pulled off below and stopped to explore. That two-hour ramble took on the contour of an allegory.

Hiking up the first ridge and gazing into the stratum, I was struck by a 180-degree sweep of flesh-colored jumble, a single organism becoming many. Beehive formations barely held together; broken columns leaned against each other for support; boulders sprawled with no plan. Rain that had slid from the rocks filled pockets between them with sharp green—paloverdes, jojoba and, because this was the topmost rung of the Upper Sonoran, the leathery beginnings of chaparral. This softening was punctuated by vegetation that seemed firmer than the rock itself, the shafts of great saguaros. A formation splintering apart, sending up numberless green lives—it was what theologians might call creation by division.

I made my way to the smooth sand at the drainage bottom, then started into the rocky panorama. There was no way to pick a route beforehand; one could only clamber from rock to rock, calculating two or three boulders ahead. The coarse granite easily held my foot treads, but granules pulverized into sand even as I climbed. My arms—atrophied as the arms of most hikers—got a workout as I hoisted myself through this stone jungle gym. Often boulders were too big, defied passage, and I had to descend here and try over there. Or I was funneled into vegetation between the rocks, where the serrated edges of barberry leaves and the spikes of yucca waited on point. Backtracking, zigzagging, I won my way to the next ridge, across a small drainage and onto the spine of the formation. The foreground of intricate granite suddenly gave way to vast distance. Low clouds hung over peaks luminous with fresh snow; far darkening relieved busy foreground. As I caught my breath, a clatter burst beneath me, and I spun in time to watch a four-point stag bound through the very rocks I'd been threading. I followed the ridge in a kind of exaltation, watching the stone labyrinth fall beneath me as hanging clouds heightened the far mountains. I came to a virtually boulder-free fold that escorted me back to the main drainage, over the ridge, and I was back to the car in two hours. As I say, the ramble was like an allegory, though fortunately there was no one around to tell me what it meant.

Once I had sampled the place on foot, I made time for exploration every time I passed. I hiked it from the top down as well as from the bottom up, at different times of day. I became familiar with topography that always sprang surprises. I saw clumps of hedgehog cactus whose tips had been eaten by javelinas, the pulp gone, the spines and skin strewn like fast-food wrappers. A saguaro had a wraparound lower limb like a skater descending into a sit spin. There were cardinals, the relatively uncommon ladderback woodpecker, and one day I flushed a great horned owl. After a February storm I came upon a freestanding granite basin cupping melted snow, so symmetrical it could have been commissioned with tax dollars. I sat and drank: the water was cool, bland, sublime.

Sated with rocks, I became aware of the way moss and grasses filled their hollows, particularly on north slopes, and the way lichen covered the rocks themselves. Growth-coated rocks weren't flesh-colored at all; they were olive, baize, mustard, Day-Glo chartreuse and, more interestingly, a perfectly unreflective, eye-resistant matte black—one or more of the 120 species of *Andreaea*, commonly known as granite moss. Here and there were bright green shotgun shells and sometimes I heard shots, for no desert seems complete these days without the most dangerous predator. My winter explorations were well timed to avoid the secondmost dangerous predator, the rattlesnake, which is really only dangerous when it can't see you coming: i.e., in places like this. As the season warmed, only the open sand in the central wash would be secure from snakes, and I had already walked its length, back to the highway and underneath. The culvert was a cold plunge where dry air suddenly hung dank, my footsteps rang from all directions, and pupils tightened by bright granite were unmoored by concentric rings where corrugated iron caught the far sky.

Most of all, I liked to sit on the first ridge as day declined and rocks leapt forward as individuals from their shadows. I could rehearse the way granite cooled and hardened from magma beneath the surface. Tectonic forces lifted it, exposed it, relieved it of subterranean pressure. It cracked along perpendicular faults. The outer surface of the rock dried rapidly after rain and snow, but moisture that seeped inside was caught until decay set in. Layers peeled off in the unsheathing of exfoliation, also known as spalling and spheroidal weathering. Lichen, the first plant to colonize land, clung to the layers as they fell, perhaps even helped them go. Here, in this vegetal transition zone, where cactus mingled with chaparral, was a geological transition zone, rock released into sand. Just as a spring is a course for water, so is disbanded rock, for a desert, pure source.

Staring until I had only enough dusk to find my way out, I liked to imagine the whole formation disintegrating under the moon, in darkness, offering new soil at first light. No other corner I know of so merits some lines I remember from Robinson Jeffers:

> *I have seen the dust on a summer day*
> *Crying to be born as much as flesh*
> *Ever cried to be quiet.*

IT HAS NEVER BEEN adequately explained why environmentalists and research scientists tend to an interest in music, particularly classical music, wildly surpassing probability. Physicists at universities and laboratories across the country regularly meet to read through scores and give chamber recitals. *Not Man Apart*, the publication of Friends of the Earth, has noted with awe the number of environmentalists who are part-time musicians. Many immersed in abstract theory relax by playing with the local symphony, or by listening to extensive record collections, and almost emblematic is the figure of Einstein, who insisted on playing, however badly, the violin. A certain correlation would be anticipated because of educational levels and the cultural matrix, but why music in particular, in such percentages, with such fanaticism?

Music seems to inhabit the mercurial dark at the human

Science,
Environmentalism,
and Music

center, and the ability of patterned sound to become charged with our feeling is an enigma that still ends, like music itself, in silence. For kinds of music that appeal to the brain as well as the bone to be pleasurable to certain kinds of people is less mysterious. Some hidden bond must link the scientist and the environmentalist with the musician—a bond which I believe to be their common rage for systems.

Consider the infant just learning to walk. His humanity is already absorbed in the process of distinguishing self from nonself, and sorting the nonself into dog, chair, Mama, food, caca. At the same time he is abstracting those externals into some interior system of words. If Noam Chomsky is right, words themselves, regardless of culture, await a built-in syntax, some master language within which all languages fall. Just as the seed is coded with the plant, the human brain is ripe with the patterns that will bloom into the human complexity. We are from birth spinners of systems.

Systemizing proceeds through stages. Between first grammar and adolescence comes the acquisitive stage, one which many of us never leave. It is the dread age of collecting: rocks, coins, stamps, model planes, baseball cards. As adults we may substitute antiques, African violets or pornography, but the unstated goal is still the same: when the collection is complete, one has all of one's chosen category. Life in its extravagance is too vast for possession, but the collector can isolate some element small enough for purchase. Any collection expanding toward its goal of completeness gives the satisfaction of an acquired language, a new system.

With adolescence and adulthood come new levels of abstraction. Now it is perhaps a passion for maps, for visiting all the National Parks or Wilderness Areas, for reading all of one author, for photographing the highlights of one's travels or one's life, for amassing friends, money, votes, sexual conquests. Systems become less an array of objects than a rainbow of memories and achievements intended to give pleasure across the spectrum. That it does not is irrelevant; the joy is to proceed.

At the highest system-gathering short of mystical fusion, the mind seeks to understand the relation of each component to its fellows so as to grasp how a system adapts, evolves and survives as a breathing creature. At this point one turns into an economist, an astronomer, a biologist, a physicist, a student of politics, anthropology, ecosystems, medicine or the law. With sufficient brass one becomes an expert. In mankind's eyes, and particularly one's own, one has reached an enviable plateau; one has captured a system alive.

To fuse our amateur musicians, the abstract scientist and the environmentalist, consider what the brain faces trying to absorb a single ecosystem. It begins over like a child, isolating and naming the parts: microbes, insects, plants, mammals, the airborne and the aquatic, all animal and vegetable organisms and everything in between. Next the burden of assembly: How does it relate to its context in the mineral world? What are the food chains? How does it divide up territory? How does it adapt to changes in climate, sudden gaps in the food chain, blooms and eclipses of species, the rise of one form and decline of another? What, indeed, are the variables? Most fiendishly, how does it perceive itself? One must consider that many organisms are blind, react only to variations in temperature, see only in two dimensions or in shades of gray, possess hearing or scent or sight keener than our own, or have senses like sonar which we lack entirely. No creature may be aware that other creatures perceive it at all, yet their exclusive realities meld into a fabric with its own dynamics of organization, change and endurance—a superorganism that sustains itself perhaps blindly but correctly. Aldo Leopold enjoined his fellow forest rangers, before they meddled with their territories, to "think like a mountain." Good but impossible advice: with perception splintered into as many modes as there are species, only God, if he so chose, could think like a mountain. It seems clear that anyone who tackles one of the abstract sciences feels impelled to take systemizing to the limit. The task is necessarily hopeless, for the physicist as well as the ecologist. The variables themselves are too numerous to be identified. Our knowledge of them comes through five senses as arbitrary and isolated as those of any other creature, or from the sense-extending machines that have blossomed since the Renaissance. For the student of ecology the task involves sensibilities that are alien and inaccessible, and for the physicist a range from the infinitesimal to the cosmic that baffles the human scale. There is the further limitation of our imagination, well expressed by the physicist who said that "the universe is not only queerer than we suppose, but queerer than we can suppose." The apprehension of any transhuman system is a mirage that flees geometrically as one approaches.

Complete knowledge of a system, then, can only be possible under one condition—that it be wholly human in origin. Yet many such systems exist. Spun by the human imagination out of the shapes, colors, sounds, solids and spaces of this world, out of the languages of word, number and tone, and out of our sense of proportion, they are the arts. Unless experimentally computed for randomness, art depends upon choice, deliberate or unconscious, by the human brain upon materials to hand. Each category of art, within the limitations of its medium and its rules to be followed or broken, is its own system, accessible because it is secreted out of ourselves.

And of all the arts, music is the most transparent to pure

form. Upon our emotions it is the most direct. At times it almost demands that we move in time, be carried along, ride its melodic crests and step to its rhythms. It will not let go of our memories. Yet even as music insists through our blood it permits us to wield our intelligence upon its relation of parts, its symmetries and oppositions, its unfolding balance. To thread the labyrinth any composer sets off produces a mental exhilaration that runs parallel to, but is distinct from, the raw sweep of emotion.

The composer is the quintessential creator of systems. It is his province to produce the most perfect, or the grandest, or the most exquisitely chiseled construct of which he is capable, whether song, sonata or symphony. He may not rationally understand how a certain passage came to be, just as artists in all fields have attested to the sensation of creation simply coming *through* them, but the greater the composer, the more mysterious the ease with which he will satisfy and still surprise—and the greater the challenge to the listener. "Music is feeling, then, not sound," says Wallace Stevens; "You are the music while the music lasts," says T. S. Eliot. Music allows you to be a system even as you trace its whorls and reversals.

Like the child, like the ecologist, the listener begins in ignorance, a strand at a time: the notes of a phrase, the phrases of a melody, the overlapping of melodies, the harmonies that engender further elaborations—music's atoms and galaxies, its spiraling energy, its explosions, its mass and empty space, its organizing gravity. The viola in a quartet, a horn passage in a symphony, a recurrent or fleeting motif, a strand of polyphony among many—in the community of systems these are the dolphins that leap through the current, the keening of the hawk, the nibblers among roots, and the great winged migrations. Struggling for dominance, harmonizing in symbiosis, working its destiny in baroque stasis, in romantic evolution or in contemporary leaps and gaps—each factor unraveling as if unaware of its place in the composite—music is the career of a complete organism, its adaptations, its disappearances, its summits and its final silence. Yet music is also the product of a single human brain, and offers the listener a single statement. Perhaps what is so satisfying to the physicist, the astronomer, the outdoor enthusiast, the seeker of wholes—and the final seduction of music—is this: music is not a system of objects, but a paradigm of systems. It satisfies the cerebral hunger even as it engages our deepest feelings.

Music as a metaphor for existence, of course, is no novelty. Pythagoras took it quite literally, and when he found that the division of vibrating strings by whole numbers created the sounds most harmonious to the ear, believed he had decoded creation's own harmony. The Ptolemaic system sang those harmonies with crystal spheres. Myths in which Orpheus creates harmony out of chaos parallel the division of light from darkness, the firmament from the waters, in a kind of musical Genesis.

The musical universe did not die with Copernicus. In the twentieth century Rilke based his personal mysticism on Orphic myths and Eliot shaped his in musical form with the *Four Quartets*. The composer Scriabin believed he discovered a musical symmetry in the bisected octave—the augmented fourth or flatted fifth—and his converts have attested to experiencing through his music a blinding white light and other transcendent phenomena. Claude Lévi-Strauss, whose *Le Cru et le Cuit* is based like the Eliot poems on musical forms, has said that to think mythologically is to think musically. There are books expounding the Symphony of Life, and the possibilities of metaphoric degeneration are as available as bad music itself.

But most significantly for us there is contemporary physics with its great cosmic and subatomic patterns, its evolving symmetries of quarks and neutrinos, the double helix of molecular biology, all the spiraling configurations of matter, which is, as it turns out, interchangeable with energy. The universe, says Sir James Jeans, begins to resemble a gigantic thought—and, one might almost add, a musical thought.

But it is a thought most of us will never think. Hiking the ecosystem with cameras and guidebooks, listening to recordings, shuffling through chaos with our five thin senses, most of us feel clever enough just to find the trail. We look up and promptly forget the names of our fellow coordinates until the next time they bloom or sting us or fly past. We listen to Brahms, relishing but not quite grasping how a passage, satisfactory in passing, answers to the whole. But once in a while our binoculars catch an oriole braiding its nest out of a fan palm, or hear in the second theme a slow inversion of the first. Those insights tell us little more than the data they connect, but they offer just the exhilaration, the sense of penetration, which is joy in the mind.

To reproduce the universe inside, in imitation of our gods, is our upward mobility. Human intelligence, divine theft that it is, is still isolated and frail, its patterns only tentative. But those systems are vital to consciousness as we know it, and as the only species so obsessed, we are the music while the music lasts.

UNLIKELY VECTORS HAD CONVERGED. The Russian poet Joseph Brodsky was in town for a few days in the summer of June 1991, as guest of the Aspen Writers' Foundation, and the mayor had proclaimed a Joseph Brodsky Day. I never determined why Brodsky was singled out for this honor, since no previous visiting writer had been, Brodsky had no special connection to Aspen, and Nobel laureates were a common migratory species. I was, for that matter, standing in line with one on the lawn of the Aspen Historical Society as I waited to get my Brodsky collection signed. The physicist Murray Gell-Mann, inventor of quark theory, was an old friend and travelmate with whom I had recently spent a couple of weeks in Oaxaca and Chiapas searching for quetzals and other exotic avifauna. Murray was on the board of the MacArthur Foundation, which had recently awarded Brodsky one of its lavish grants. "I've

Arrows of Time

just given Brodsky a half-million dollars," said Murray with mock testiness, rolling the *r* and deepening the *o* in the Russian manner. "I assume he'll sign my book."

After we had scored our signatures, Murray remarked, "I'm headed to a physics conference in Spain next month. Why don't you come with me?" I almost didn't hear him because I was laughing at what Brodsky had written in my book. Above his name on the title page he had scrawled the line my father loved to crow when he was dealer in poker: *Read 'em and weep!* "The conference is on the arrow of time and there are lots of fancy people, but that's not the interesting part," Murray was saying. "It takes place at a town called Mazagón, on the edge of the Coto Doñana. I can get us permission to go into the coto. In the other direction is prime habitat for the great bustard. The conference is five days long and we could extend it by showing up three days early, to explore the area."

Murray was aware of my failed connection to the Coto Doñana. For three years during the mid-sixties I had lived near the edge of this royal hunting ground in the delta of the Rio Guadalquivir. The map had not identified what it was. A large triangle empty of towns, it was merely marked *marisma*, marshland, and flecked with a few schematic weeds. The effect was mysterious, and as friends and I gaped across the unbridged Guadalquivir at the uninhabited far bank from the town of Sanlúcar de Barrameda, I pressed for details. "It's just swamp," they answered with finality.

Shortly after I returned to the States, in 1968, James Michener published a nonfiction work called *Iberia*, devoting a chapter to this swamp. It was the most important stop for migrating birds on the flyway between wintering grounds in Africa and summer nesting terrain in Eurasia from Scotland to Siberia, a kind of migrational funnel for hundreds of species.

For centuries the traditional hunting ground of Spanish royalty, with a recreational palace in its midst, it had been turned in the mid-sixties into a biological reserve—the most important one in Europe. I read it and wept. On a return visit in the late eighties I had taken advantage of the only visitation open to the public, boarding a large Land Rover with a few other sign-ups. The tour lasted three hours, the car windows were too smudged to see out of, the guide had no information, we were let out at a couple of dull and birdless spots, and I felt I had been subjected to an ill-spliced home movie. But now I was practically commuting to Spain, having become a contributing editor at *American Way*, the magazine of American Airlines. I had written for them on art in Madrid, on offshore banking in Gibraltar, on changes in the obscure town I used to live in. Physics conferences weren't normal fodder for in-flight magazines but *American Way* was going through an improbable literary phase, evidenced by the fact that my co-editors included Wallace Stegner and Ray Bradbury.

"I'm planning to fly American," said Murray.

"So am I," I replied. "On American's nickel."

WHEN MURRAY AND I converged at Dallas–Fort Worth, he with a first-class ticket and I with a tourist-class seat supplied by the magazine, Murray scowled at my clothing. "If you're traveling first class," he pronounced, "you can wear what you like, but if you're traveling tourist you should wear a coat and tie."

I hadn't expected to be baffled until the conference. "Why is that?"

"Because if you want to be bumped up to first class, you have to look as if you belong there. Wait here." He marched to the first-class desk in his crisp gray suit and returned. "It's arranged. You're sitting with me."

I marveled at how swiftly the Atlantic Ocean passed beneath us: what with the conversation and first-class wines, we were already circling Barajas, the Madrid airport, where we would change to a short flight to Seville. But the arrival itself seemed long. We were still circling when the voice of the pilot came on: the Madrid radar was broken and we were flying to Málaga to refuel. We spent an hour on the Málaga runway and Murray asked if we couldn't get off and rent a car. "Not if you want your luggage," snapped the flight attendant. By the time we returned to Madrid, our connecting flight had gone. We waited two hours and got the last flight to Seville. Finally into our rental car, we found that Seville was torn up for next year's Expo, part of the quincentennial celebration of the Spanish discovery of America, and I couldn't find our way out of town. We reached the parador, the inn at Mazagón, well after midnight—eight in the evening by our own clocks—and were commanded to be ready for our expedition to the Coto Doñana before dawn.

IT WAS STILL DARK when we were being driven to the Coto Doñana by the Spanish physicist Juan Perez-Mercader, the conference's compact and energetic organizer. "The park's proximity to the conference is nonrandom," he stated. Juan had grown up in the nearby city of Huelva and was, like us, an avid birder. Doñana, off-limits now to even royal hunting as well as to development, provided little employment and antagonized the local population. "Doñana is in the headlines for the wrong reasons. I've arranged for the physicists to take an afternoon off to tour the park. When it becomes clear that well-known scientists could have an event like this essentially anywhere, but pick this place because it is near a beautiful nature reserve, it brings home to people in Spain that Doñana is valuable. We Spaniards are as provincial as anyone else. We don't value what we have until people from the outside value it first." I mentioned that Michener valued it but also predicted in 1968 that, due to development, the marisma would be dry by 1985. "Good," Juan replied. "Michener was wrong."

By the time we arrived at a locked gate, the day was breaking into a tangerine shimmer. Juan ordered the guard to open. As the grillwork swung, Murray pronounced, "I have waited for this moment for decades." To voice my own emotion would only have sounded like "Me, too," so I assented silently.

"I have a conference to organize, so I'm turning you over to Rodolfo," said Juan, and we climbed into a Land Rover owned by the coto. Its windows were sparkling.

I had expected to be plunged into a marsh loud with birdsong but we inched along a gravel road across a series of dry lakebeds populated with standing cattle. The intervening hills appeared cropped to the bone. Single trees spiked the horizon, and though the day was mild enough, warming air from the hardpan trembled them to smoke. Red-legged partridges ran in coveys beside us. I asked Rodolfo why there were cows. "We eliminated them at one point and wound up with less diversity than we have now. We decided a controlled herd is beneficial and it makes us less unpopular with the people here."

"Stop," interjected Murray, bailing out with binoculars and a black leather case containing recording equipment around his neck. He returned to the car a few moments later and punched PLAY. Birdsong filled the car. "It's a crested lark," said Murray.

It was the amplified echo of a cry we had heard far off, one that had barely registered, and it struck me that tape recorders were binoculars for ears.

The lakebed gave way to expanses of marsh grass flecked with pine groves and scattered dunes, calm as a sky with cirrus feathering. Trees gathered to a density at a couple of low buildings and a skeletal iron tower. We climbed set after set of metal stairs through a stand of eucalyptus, up through peeling bark, stippled light and the odor of menthol to an observation platform over the treetops. From here we could appreciate the stunning flatness of the Guadalquivir delta, tawny and scribbled with watercourses in the early light. To one side stood the hunting palace used by the Spanish nobility since the fifteenth century, a two-story tile-roofed white building as unimposing as any other feature of this even terrain. The coto was like a formal demonstration that God was in the details.

We returned to the Rover and continued in and among. The very flatness made the country mysterious, secretive of its riches, though now and then a CB radio crackled to life as biologists kept track of the biota and one another. We wound on single-lane tracks through grasslands, past well-spaced cork oaks. When we stopped to peer at ponds through binoculars, we saw herons, storks and flamingos—blurred, on occasion, by the passing antlers of red deer—while past the life-forms drifted sand in clouds of buff. We stopped at reed enclosures with eye-level slits and surveyed pools with avocets, ringed plovers and that globe-encompassing duck, the mallard. We stopped at a research station where several young people were banding small black-and-russet birds, temporarily in cages. "The Dartford warbler was named for the little town where they were first found in England," Murray told them in Spanish.

"Which is ironic," replied a bander, "since they are rare in England and common here."

"They're ground feeders, frequently killed on the highway," added another bander, and to demonstrate he slid one from an envelope, saying that he had picked it up that morning while driving to work.

When we continued, Murray heard the high-flown whoops of a pin-tailed sandgrouse. Could he see the bird on the ground? Our guide radioed biologists to ask where the pin-tailed sandgrouse had last been sighted and we gave chase, tracking it down near a pine grove. The shade provided just the spot to attack our box lunches from the parador. We still hadn't caught sight of the bird Murray most wanted to see. Where, he demanded, was the azure-winged magpie? Rodolfo replied that the magpie could be glimpsed on foot, but only in rapid flight from the observer. Murray wolfed his lunch and set off at a brisk pace to pursue magpies. It was a good moment to learn something of Rodolfo. Where was he from?

"The nearest town. It's called El Rocío."

"El Rocío! I was there for three days once." It was the spring of 1967, when I was living in Puerto de Santa María, twenty kilometers from the other side of the Guadalquivir. El Rocío was the location of the annual celebration of the Virgin of El Rocío, La Paloma Blanca, who was shouldered drunkenly through the revelers at the climax of a three-day binge. Each town in that part of Andalucía had an *hermandad*, a small empty building where people could throw blankets and sleeping bags and set up their butane burners, anything to keep the body together while the soul went on a debauch. The *hermandades* were laid out in streets but I thought of it as a kind of camp, a Potemkin village, not a town someone could actually be from. Besides wanting to experience this blowout of dancing and flamenco fomented by gypsies, I had also hoped to attack the map's blank spot from another direction. Perhaps I could ditch the melee and just walk into the marisma from the other side. Gazing in that direction, all I saw were plain fields and trees. I confessed to Rodolfo that his hometown to me was a kind of stage set remembered in a drunken blur.

"You were at El Rocío the event, not El Rocío the town."

"It was enough of an event that I was even baptized. A priest no more sober than I was asked if I had been. I told him I grew up in a Protestant sect that didn't baptize, but I reassured him that I didn't believe in Protestantism either. He told me I was marked for damnation but he could fix it on the spot. He poured wine on my head, made the sign of the cross and gave me a name. If there is a Catholic afterlife, I will be known for eternity as José y María del Rocío."

"You and several thousand others."

"It beats burning in hell. But you mean El Rocío is a real town?"

"I'm a schoolteacher there, but I found unexpected work in the coto. I love birds. To be honest, I love birds more than I love schoolchildren. I'm trying to learn all the species."

"What do people in El Rocío think of the Coto Doñana?"

"I've been attacked in bars for working here. Just last week someone threw stones at the car of another employee. A strawberry-growing operation just started near here, a complicated business involving special fertilizers and plastic cover. When a crop failed because of bad management, they blamed it on this place. 'Doñana took the water.' They had plenty of water and none of it went to the coto. They don't like the idea of this place, the notion that there's something near them that's set aside for protection instead of production, so when something totally unconnected goes wrong for any reason, they blame it on the Coto Doñana. It's an all-purpose scapegoat. But as far as I'm concerned, the pleasure of working in Doñana outweighs the abuse. Also, as a local I have plenty of help in the bars. I'm from this place as much as the people who don't like the coto."

Murray returned, complaining that he had caught no sight of the azure-winged magpie, and we circled back to the observation tower. We paused at park headquarters to meet the assistant director, who gave me a pass to come back and talk to him at more leisure, should I wish to—then, to my excitement, we proceeded to the royal hunting palace. More like a swollen country house, it was furnished with long tables and heavy chairs that suggested feasting. The only wall adornments were black-and-white photographs of the formerly famous, mostly royal and cinematic, posing with felled animals and one another. Like everything else in the Coto Doñana it was straightforward, unimposing, but when we wrote our names in the guest book, it felt like we were signing history.

DESPITE A CONFERENCE to prepare, Juan drove us the following day to view the highly endangered European black vulture. As we approached the town of Moguer, I remarked that it was the setting of the first book I had read in Spanish, Juan Ramón Jiménez's *Platero y yo*. Juan was soon pointing out the car window. "That pine is the subject of one of its chapters." I noted its location so I could return to it alone during some break in the conference.

We stopped in a town called Zalamea la Real to pick up a balding and energetic man named Ricardo, a close friend of Juan's, and began to climb over back roads. The pines around us were aligned in rows, all the same height. Why the tree farm? I asked. Twenty years ago the oak forest had been leveled, and an entire ecosystem destroyed, so that the slopes could be planted with eucalyptus, a disastrous Australian import sown worldwide for cellulose. Now they wanted the ecosystem back. There was no way to re-create the original complex forest, but the best alternative was to re-establish its predominant tree, the cork oak, and welcome whatever grew beneath it in hopes that a new and complex equilibrium would establish itself. The cork oak, however, got started only in the shade of other trees, and these fast-growing, temporary pines were providing the necessary cover. Leveling the original forest with an eye toward profit had proved a disaster even financially, for the recovery plan was far more costly than the original conversion to eucalyptus.

Miraculously, a vestige of the original habitat remained up top—some towering pines, two species of heather, and the black vultures. There was no need to look for them, for they had nowhere else to go. Planing against some incoming clouds, holding their place while the wind tore beneath them, they were a calm, self-adjusting, gale-breasting awareness. Said Ricardo, "During the forties, when Stalin was still alive and Russian passports weren't honored in Spain, I knew a Russian who came here illegally because there were similar birds in Russia and watching these kept him sane. We met up here, because I was doing the same thing. I was furious during the Franco era and I kept my sanity by watching the black vultures. Look at the way they make no effort to climb or descend, but neither are they ever quite motionless. They ride the wind and go where they want by endless small adjustments, by independently altering the position of each wing and by fanning and shrinking the tail. To watch them is infinitely calming."

A DESERT HARVEST

All the conference participants had been sent a request sheet and Murray had written that he wished to see a great bustard. Inspired that carrion-eaters had taught a man to ride out a dictatorship, I had hoped some similar revelation would emerge from the following day's search for a twenty-pound game bird—but Juan could not take another day off from the conference and Murray realized that he was programmed to give a forty-minute presentation, "Quantum Cosmology and the Arrow of Time," and had made no preparatory notes. We drove, indeed, into bustard terrain but I, at the wheel, didn't know what to look for and let my eyes wander the rolling fields of olives while Murray, in the passenger seat, applied pen to paper. Now and then I glanced in Murray's lap and found his notebook filling with a cuneiform scribble of words, numbers and arcane symbols. Having sighted no twenty-pound game birds, we pulled into the parador as workmen were erecting a huge sign that said, in English, PHYSICAL ORIGINS OF TIME ASYMMETRY. Beyond them, calmly feeding on the lawn, was a flock of azure-winged magpies. This bird that Murray had pursued in vain through the Coto Doñana turned out to be as common at the Parador de Mazagón as the robin is on an American campus.

UNDER NO ILLUSION that I would understand the conference, I had nonetheless read up. I was aware of updated notions about time. The medium of communication in the universe, for instance, was light. The order in which packets of light reached you made up the sequence of events for you, though some light reached you almost instantaneously while other light had been traveling toward you since the birth of the universe. Light from the sun, for instance, gave news of what happened eight minutes ago whereas light from a quasar was billions of years old. As we go through our daily lives, there are nanoseconds of difference in the arrival times of light from any source, including one another, so that at an imperceptible level we are all marooned in our own time. At the galactic scale the disparities become huge, giving far-flung observers different sequences, different histories of the universe.

As for the arrow of time, the order in which things happen, observation and common sense find a simple one-way street. We remember the past and anticipate the future. The wineglass falls and shatters. It is hard to imagine a sequence in which pieces of the wineglass spontaneously reassemble themselves and leap back onto the table. An irreversibility—or time asymmetry, or arrow of time—is implied by the smashed glass. The event moves only in one direction. But at the level of the quantum, the behavior of the elementary particles that make up the universe, there was in fact nothing to prevent the smashed crystal from reassembling into a wineglass. Individual particles are quite free to reverse course, and for them to do so individually or collectively breaks no laws of physics. Their failure to do so—ever—was only a statistical improbability. Billions of particles would have to do just the right thing at the right time to reconstruct the wineglass, and for that possibility to come up among the trillions of alternatives would take many multiples of the estimated timespan of the universe to date. Due to the probabilities, an arrow of time at the macro level of the wineglass kept the crystal in pieces—and kept people from rising from the grave—but at the level of the elementary particles, where the mechanics of the quantum prevailed, any combination was possible and the arrow of time seemed to disappear.

Then there was the truly big picture, where three arrows of time were generally conceded to be pointing in the same direction. The cosmological arrow was the well-known expansion of the universe. The thermodynamic arrow, less easy to picture, was the universe's increasing disorder as it expanded. This was the famous Second Law of Thermodynamics, or the increase of entropy in a closed system. The universe was in its highest state of order at the moment of the Big Bang and had been growing more disordered ever since. It's hard to grasp that this decline coincides with the generation of stars and the evolution of life, but the physicists explain that these organizational processes throw off heat that increases the overall disorder of the universe, and the law of entropy is not violated. Finally there is the psychological arrow, the one we all understand: on Monday we are invited to a party and, come Tuesday, we party.

Much of this speculation about the arrows of time was concerned with how they got launched. Did they start from a singularity called the Big Bang, or did they emerge from a relatively smooth initial condition without a boundary as proposed by co-theorists Jim Hartle and Stephen Hawking, both present at the conference? Would the universe reach a limit of expansion and begin to contract, and if so, would that reverse all the arrows of time? Theories of the remote beginning and end were in perpetual flux and my mind was in a swirl, with strains of these notions floating about in increasing disorder. I did know that it was between the initial expansion and ultimate dissipation that stars, galaxies and planets like our own were created. Conditions were ripe for what Murray called complex adaptive systems—and the rest of us called life-forms—to be generated all over the universe. I was most interested in this transition period, this precious few billion years when physicists generated conferences on the arrow of time and azure-winged magpies walked on the lawn.

The gathering's opening statement was made by John Wheeler, a revered physicist in his eighties, who began, "We are holding this conference just twenty-three kilometers from where Columbus, four hundred and ninety-nine years ago, left on his first voyage to the New World." The hotel that rambled neocolonially around us was called, in fact, the Parador Cristóbal Colón—Christopher Columbus Inn. Despite the symbolism that physicists, half a millennium later, were embarking on their own journey of discovery, that was the last reference to the iconic Columbus.

Wheeler's "How Come Time?" was the first of forty presentations over the next five days, each lasting twenty to forty minutes. Eight long tables, each with six seats, filled a room semi-darkened for a lighted screen, and each place was provisioned with a bottle of mineral water and a glass. Physicists, in slacks and jeans, sport shirts and sweaters, came and went at will, but nearly a full quorum of fifty people attended each talk. Only one of these physicists was female and only a handful of males brought their wives. Only Murray showed up with a non-spouse, making me a category of one.

The talks unfolded on two tracks at once, for a projector picked up handwritten transparencies of statements and equations and threw them onto the screen, supporting or modifying the verbal delivery. Sometimes the speakers laid a second transparency in a different color over the first, amplifying the possibilities, and sometimes they began by showing only the top, then slowly revealed the rest of the transparency as they developed their theme, a process known as a striptease. Because all talks were in English, the visuals were no doubt crucial to physicists from Russia, India, Japan, Brazil and a half-dozen other countries—but they were also a help to English-speakers coping with references to cirkwits and trayectories as difficult concepts fought their way through non-English tongues. I hung on the screen for any help it could give me with such presentations as "Fluctuation-Dissipation in Quantum Fields and Gravitational Entropy" and "Time (A-)Symmetry in Recollapsing Quantum Universe." And sometimes there were better visuals out the windows to one side, where pines mindlessly drank the sun.

Unable to follow the presentations despite the heavy reading, I jotted down phrases. "Time is hidden among the cosmic variables." "The conceptual scheme of physical objects is a convenient myth, of which time is a scattered part." "Nature incontinently copies information, and that is the origin of irreversibility." At one point I retreated to the men's room and heard a physicist say, "Am I confused or is he confused? If all three vectors have the same trajectory, don't they . . ."

"Stop!" snapped the man at the adjoining urinal. "I got confused long before that."

Back in the conference room I heard a physicist remark, "I've asked the desk to confirm my airline tickets, and that in itself implies an undeniable flow of time." I shot him an appreciative look. That arrow was in my own quiver. And don't forget the party on Tuesday.

All of this abstraction surrounded the strangest of spectacles, the presence of Stephen Hawking. During the preceding days, as Murray and I commuted to the birds, we had watched local workmen constructing a ramp along the stairs to the conference room. In the advanced stages of amyotrophic lateral sclerosis, known to Americans as Lou Gehrig's disease, this man who had devoted his career to black-hole theory was confined to a wheelchair. During the first morning he glided quietly into his place at the center of the back row, with two nurses hovering behind him. His vehicle, with its high back and wings around Hawking's head, resembled a diminutive men's club chair. Dense with machinery that included a rectangular box along the back, another underneath, wires, tubes and bits of luminous tape, it looked like the upshot of high tinkering. The occupant, with his large eyes and full mouth, might have been unusual-looking without the disease; now almost lacking substance, he generally sat sideways with his legs crossed, his mouth open and fallen to one side, asymmetry made flesh. Because physics is an attempt to explain everything, and its themes saturated five strenuous days, it was hard not to see Hawking through the lens of his own theory. He was imploding toward some final opacity.

Partial motion in his left hand allowed him two-fingered operation of a control panel that moved his chair and programmed his artificial voice. He moved his fingers and speech sounds, not his native British but an American, National Public Radio enunciation, emanated from somewhere beneath him. Particularly grating was the word *to*, which came out *tuh*, a calculated folksiness. Long sits in the chair apparently exhausted him—or the presentations bored him—for he often returned to his room. When he needed to move between floors, he and his vehicle parted company, for the chair was dense as a neutron star and it took several strong men to push it up the ramp or restrain it on the downhill. The nurses carried Hawking himself as if he were weightless, a limp child who sometimes cradled his head against them. He was Pascal's figure of man, a thinking reed.

Because black holes had seized the popular imagination as metaphors as well as objects, and because their famous theo-

rist had lived three times longer with amyotrophic lateral sclerosis than any other known sufferer, Hawking was treated by
the outside world as the star of the conference. Regional newspapers didn't reach Mazagón but they were said to be full of
Stephen Hawking; whether reporters could communicate with
him or not, he was the man they wanted to meet. Meaning no
disrespect but maintaining perspective, some of the other physicists referred to his presence as the Stephen Show. As a scientist, they considered him merely a bright mind among bright
minds. The Nobel committee had never awarded him the prize
despite an annual opportunity to do so. His theory for the origin of time was, properly, the Hartle-Hawking No Boundary
Proposal, and I had known his collaborator, Jim Hartle, socially through Murray for years, finding him a normal person
by physicist standards. The man Murray singled out to me was
not Stephen Hawking but the aging John Wheeler, who had
given the first presentation. "You don't appreciate who he is,
but you need to meet him anyway," said Murray one day, leading me to him just to shake his hand. The Stephen Show added
a very strange note to the conference, but it was finally just
one note in the larger polyphony.

BY THE THIRD AFTERNOON it was a relief to forsake quantum
decoherence for a tour of the Parque Doñana. Murray took a
dim view of invading the marisma with fifty other physicists,
particularly after our day of roaming at will, then succumbed
when he realized we would be touring a beach with three rare
gulls. A huge bus deposited us at the park's public headquarters—
prematurely, it seemed, for no one was in charge to tell us
what to do next. Most of the physicists were still talking about
irreversibility and the inflationary scenario rather than looking

around. Familiar with the site, Murray and I took off down a trail. Spotting directional behavior, the entire party charged in our wake toward the blind. Soon the little house of rushes, outfitted with stools and a strip of air to look through, was filled with some seventy people craning around one another five deep for ten or fifteen minutes, peering for a glimpse of some mallards and the odd egret. The sights exhausted, the party trooped back to the parking lot, where the arriving guides wondered how so many physicists had managed to pour out of a bus and escort themselves.

We transferred to smaller and squarish olive-drab buses, took off like a military convoy and cruised along the beach without spotting the rare gulls. We turned inland and were let out on the highest dune. Below us were red and fallow deer, along with scattered bones. "It's the remains of the last party of physicists," said a man with a Slavic accent. We wound back past ponds and pine groves, but with most birds dormant mid-afternoon, it was hard to know whether Doñana was making an impression. Curious for an opinion on whether the conference was helping Doñana, I skipped next morning's lectures, "Quantum Cryptology" and "Fluctuation-Dissipation and the Cosmological Constant," and returned to park headquarters to talk with Eduardo Crespo, the park's assistant director.

Young, engaged and voluble, Crespo launched into his explanation. "Spain is the jewel in Western Europe as far as natural heritage is concerned. Sixty years ago, the wetland in the delta was six times larger than it is now. The problem is that most of it was turned into rice paddies. We try to shrink human impact and keep the system close to what it was before agriculture, but we're decades from turning rice crops back into natural marshes."

When I mentioned my less rewarding visit a few years

back, he replied, "Tourist visits have nothing to do with park administration. We leave that to a concessionaire. Our first obligation is to preserve the natural and historical values, and public use is a distant second. We only handle special visits, like this conference, and as you can probably tell, it's not our forte. I'm not going to tell anyone to turn around and walk home, but we're not interested in promoting visitation."

I wondered at the insularity and mentioned that Rodolfo had been personally attacked because he worked in the coto. "Rocks have been thrown at cars. Our fire-extinguishing trucks were burned last year. There's graffiti on the walls against me and others, despite the fact that we employ hundreds of people, have environmental programs for two thousand kids in the area, and do try to reach out to local people. They have the idea that if the park weren't here, the marisma would be saturated with moneymaking apartments. Simultaneously they believe that the park exists today because they have preserved it through the centuries. Nobody has thought of things like horseback tours, nature-directed experiences, ecotourism. They can't conceive of making a profit from anything that isn't developed. Doñana will not survive if the economies in the towns don't survive, but any tampering with the park has to be very careful."

"With all this pressure, will the water hold out?"

"Too many people think the marshes are in danger of drying out forever. That's not true. There's the risk of overexploiting the water table, which would affect the ecosystem, but the marsh depends on rain and surface water, the top layer, not the bottom one."

"James Michener thought it would dry up in twenty years."

"It will fill in with sediment in four hundred years."

"Does it help to have something like the physics conference here, to draw attention to the park?"

"We don't really need publicity. Human pressure is already strong enough and, as you know, the present government spends the month of August here, which is a huge spotlight. That Stephen Hawking could help Doñana by coming here is thinking from Madrid. People in the area only appreciate what is generated locally. There are fifteen thousand people living in Almonte, the nearest sizable town, and I'm sure that fourteen thousand five hundred of them have never heard of Stephen Hawking."

I GOT BACK in time for lunch, for I was finding the meals unmissable. Three times a day, over food, physicists maintained the themes of the conference. "Computers' memories increase in the direction of entropy's increase, just like our own brains," commented one over scrambled eggs. "String theory may be elegant for physics but it's ugly for mathematics," remarked another. One lunchmate with a mouthful of sandwich mumbled something about an oscillator with an escape to minus infinity. At one point I said to Murray, as an aside, "Why not make your theories inclusive enough to embrace particles you don't believe in?" and Murray stopped the other conversations and had me repeat it as if it were some significant new principle. At the end of one particularly esoteric meal, Murray apologized, "I'm sorry this sounds so much like deconstruction."

One morning we went off of daylight savings time and there was a discussion over which way to set our watches. Did the sun rise earlier or later? I had picked up a Huelva newspaper someone had left in the lobby and showed them the pair of diagrams showing the old clock setting at ten o'clock and the new one at nine o'clock. Shortly after the watches had been set back, Jonathan Halliwell, who had given a presentation, "Time Asymmetry and Quantum Cosmology," the day before, stopped to ask, "What time is it? We've gone off of daylight savings." Murray froze. "Stop *doing* this," he said with a curt nod in my direction. "We're in front of a journalist." While I can never picture the celestial mechanics of this time change, I assumed I was among people who could—or who at least remembered the adage *spring forward, fall back*—and before bedtime I couldn't resist relishing with Murray the irony of the world's deepest thinkers about time not knowing which way to reset their watches. Murray didn't share my amusement. "It would be typical cheap journalism to use a detail like that. Journalists are always taking advantage of that kind of cliché." But my amusement persisted, particularly when a lunchmate remarked, "When I told my mother I was going to a conference on why time always runs forward, she said, 'I should have your problems.'" Today I returned from the Coto Doñana to find that Murray had saved me a place between himself and Stephen Hawking.

The experience was eerie because I could not really look at or communicate with the person at my side, though I was intensely aware of him. A nurse sat beyond him, diced vegetables and spooned them onto his tongue, where they sat open to display for a long time before they could be swallowed. Across the table was a young couple who recounted the travails of raising a two-year-old and a four-year-old. Usually I glaze at tales of child-rearing, but after so much incoherence about time it was refreshing to hear that the children had emptied a bag of flour on themselves two minutes before they were to be taken to a party, so that sponging the kids off made them late. Mainly to amuse Murray, I blurted, "Why not leave them as they were and present them as flour children?"

Murray burst out laughing, the others laughed less volubly, and, as on previous occasions, Murray initiated a discussion of why Americans often groan rather than laugh at puns. Other nationalities felt free to laugh. Was it backhanded appreciation or were Americans actually offended? As the debate proceeded, the young father saw that Hawking was fingering his panel. "I think you have something to say, Stephen," he said. Hawking gazed around the table, unswallowed vegetables piled against his bad teeth, his eyes sparkling maliciously, and from beneath him a voice like a robot through a police radio pronounced, "I am trying tuh program my synthesizer tuh groan."

By now I was attending fewer and fewer presentations, having found the Spanish of the bar far more intelligible than the English of the conference room, but I couldn't miss the presentations of lunchmates. Hawking's was called "My Greatest Mistake," an allusion to Einstein having confessed as his own greatest mistake the addition of a so-called cosmological constant to his General Theory of Relativity so as to preserve a static universe. Hawking's mistake was to believe that the arrow of time would reverse direction if the universe reached its maximum expansion and began to contract. He had been misled by certain computer solutions that had posited the wrong boundary conditions, and he had come down with pneumonia and just managed to retract the paper in question before it went out into the world. Hawking's talk had been preprogrammed on the synthesizer so that he sat at the front of the room, motionlessly facing the conferees, while the mechanical voice droned from beneath him. Partway through the talk he began to shake, then to make strange noises in the throat that simulated sobbing. Juan, the conference organizer, looked anxiously at the nurses in the back of the room, who registered no concern and seemed to be taking this convulsion for normal behavior. Hawking's spasm subsided and he resumed gazing at us impassively until the talk concluded. At the end he programmed his voice to ask for questions.

The first to volunteer was Murray. "You say that this is your biggest mistake. Are you really sure that this one is the biggest?"

Hawking's eyes sparkled; clearly he was amused rather than offended. He also declined to program a response.

THE CONFERENCE was isolated in its pines by the sea, but to make an environmental point it had been publicized and by the last day it was no secret to the outside world. Juan may have wished to elevate the popular status of the Coto Doñana, but the press didn't mob Doñana; it mobbed Stephen Hawking. Reporters and photographers, barred from the conference room, grabbed notebooks and popped flashes whenever Hawking rolled into the hall. Complained one physicist, "This is the first conference I've been to where I have to retire to my room to pick my nose."

As the guest of a participant I had not considered myself part of the media blitz, but I was unexpectedly joined by a photographer who had been assigned by *American Way* to illustrate my story. I was further stunned to learn that this photographer I'd never heard of was from my tiny hometown of Aspen, Colorado. He had just begun telling me of some unusual ideas for images when we were summoned to an official press conference by the pool. Four Spanish-speaking physicists—Juan and another Spaniard, a Portuguese and a Brazilian—were standing against the conference sign, PHYSICAL ORIGINS OF TIME ASYMMETRY, which had been removed from the front of the hotel and propped up against a chair. They gave a more lucid account of time than anything heard in the darkened room, then explained that a generation of physicists in Spain had been lost—first to the Civil War, then to the country's long isolation during the Franco dictatorship. But Spain was now in the scientific mainstream, with a conference on microbiology coming up next week in Granada, a conference on physics and music scheduled for Extremadura next summer, and many more physicists in Spain than were represented by this conference.

The group dispersed and Juan was summoned to an interview, which he gave farther up the lawn with his back to us but well within view. Would the sign float? asked the photographer. We carried it to the pool and set it gently in the water, faceup. It floated. Jeffrey wanted to shoot it lying on the surface, parallel to the poolside but slightly separated from the edge. The photograph was a Concept, one I understood no more than any other at the conference, but I saw no reason not to cooperate. I gave it a nudge and the sign blew back. I realized that the only way to control its movements was to take off my shoes and socks, roll up my pants, and give it little shoves from the pool's ladder, drawing my hand back before the camera clicked. I gave it a push, the photographer started taking pictures, it rotated and made an angle, returned, and I pushed it again. I turned around to glance at Juan, who was safely occupied by the interview. Suddenly the wind changed directions and the sign was out of reach in the middle of the pool. We began laughing uncontrollably, the photographer at the comedy, I in anxiety. Juan in his generosity had included me in the conference, gotten us privately into the Coto Doñana and taken us on an all-day expedition to the vultures in the middle of organizing a huge event. His approach to defending the coto may have differed from that of the assistant director of the preserve, but despite his alleged thinking from Madrid he was as much a native of this area as Eduardo Crespo. I would have been mortified to be caught abusing the conference sign. I glanced at Juan again and it looked like he was winding up the interview. As I rushed up the ladder and to the far side of the pool, to receive the sign or splash it back, another change of wind returned it to the edge. We fished it out with only a few water stains and propped it discreetly back against the chair.

As I walked in relief back to the parador, where Juan was indeed concluding his interview, I was intercepted by a man with a notepad. He was polling all the conferees. Did I believe or not believe in time? It was tempting to cast a vote for time and common sense but I was sure to be unmasked. "I'm not a physicist," I confessed. "I don't want to introduce noise into your survey."

I was next approached by a member of the hotel staff. I was Spanish-speaking and connected to the conference; would I come to the bar and help solve the problem of an old man from Huelva? He led me to a distinguished man in a suit jacket, whom I hadn't seen before today but whom I had noticed drinking since early in the morning. "Have a sherry," he commanded as soon as we had been introduced. When the sherries arrived, he reached into his suit jacket and pulled out a handful of postcards. He handed me the top card. I inspected a sepia shot of an old hotel. "Read the back," he said.

There was no message, only a signature. "It's a little hard to read but it looks like it says Thomas Alva Edison. Is this real?"

Without replying he took it back and handed me another. It was signed Giacomo Puccini. He handed me more in succession. None of the cards had been mailed, there were no salutations, and I didn't bother to look at the pictures. They contained the signatures of Theodore Roosevelt, Jules Massenet, Enrico Caruso and Rudyard Kipling. He spread them along the bar, reached into another pocket and unfolded some color Xeroxes. I made out the signatures of Niels Bohr, Charlie Chaplin, Richard Strauss . . . As he unfolded another page, his sleeve caught a couple of the postcards and sent them to the floor. I bent down in alarm and retrieved them, immediately checking the Edison, which had landed facedown near a puddle of beer. "You're not old enough to have gotten these yourself," I said. "Did you buy them?"

"No, no, my great-grandfather started this. My family has been collecting signatures for four generations. And we're still going. I read about the conference in yesterday's paper and got here first thing this morning. I just got Murray Gell-Mann to sign a card. Would you sign one?" From yet another pocket he pulled a postcard of the Christopher Columbus monument in Huelva and shoved a fountain pen in front of me. Inwardly laughing at the cajolery, I signed the card.

"Thank you. Bartender, two more sherries. Now I have a favor to ask. Could you get Stephen Hawking to sign a card for me?"

I suspected this might be the favor. "I'm afraid he doesn't have enough motion in his hand for that."

"But he could make a thumbprint."

Our whole conversation had been followed intensely by a shabbily dressed young man beyond the card collector and now he broke in. He had driven all the way from Galicia because he had something important to communicate to Stephen Hawking. Could I arrange it? Just as I began explaining that communication with Stephen Hawking was difficult, Hawking himself rolled past the open double door of the bar, flanked by the nurses and trailed by the media. Various times when I'd been in the bar, Hawking and the nurses on their way to and from events had created a strange vignette, and I was reminded of a cut from the film version of Graham Greene's novel of Haiti, *The Comedians*, in which Papa Doc Duvalier and retinue climb a set of stairs in the background as the plot proceeds. "Give me a card," I said to the collector. "I'll try." The young man followed me unbidden.

I caught up with one of the nurses on the veranda and explained about the card. "Stephen does sign his name with a thumbprint," she said, accepting the card without promising that Stephen would sign it. The young man kept muttering, "Introduce me," so I did so, explaining his business. She gave the Galician a business card with an address where Hawking could be contacted by mail. "People from all over the world want to contact Stephen," she said in English, which she assumed he didn't understand. "Most of them are cranks."

I was about to return to the bar when Hawking himself swooped by me onto the lawn. Suddenly he was doing turns, loops and figure eights—or perhaps they were signs of infinity—with what appeared to be sheer exuberance. If his chair had been capable of wheelies, surely he would have done them. Now physicists were pouring out of the lobby, along with chambermaids in uniform and men in chef's hats—for this was the official group photo. Several physicists arrived bearing the lobby's enormous grandfather clock, which they set next to Hawking. As flashbulbs popped and video cameras whirred, a tall physicist spun the hands of the clock backward. I was reminded that Spain had launched not only Christopher Columbus, but also Salvador Dalí.

Shortly after the photo, the poll on time came out: the conference was almost evenly split among those who believed it existed, those who didn't, and those who were undecided or had no opinion. Hawking had voted in favor of time, as had Murray, while the three conference organizers had voted against. If I had gotten away with a vote, the split would have been even. As we broke up to dress for dinner, I asked Murray what it could possibly mean when the world's leading theorists of time couldn't decide whether it existed. "The physicist who took the poll always had something against time. In any case, this poll is nonserious. When you're doing sophisticated work in the theory of gravitation and the other forces, you don't work directly with space and time coordinates but in functions of them, and space and time recede in your work." I no longer understood my own question.

The nonseriousness of the afternoon prepared us to be bused to the city of Huelva, given a reception in the hall of the provincial capital, then taken to a *peña*, or private flamenco club, for an evening of feasting and entertainment. After we had washed down heaps of shellfish with reckless changes of wine, guitarists, singers and dancers took to the stage and gave an obsessed, fixated performance. Then they invited physicists from the audience to dance with them.

I always feel deflated when artists who have shown their integrity invite burlesque, and was encouraged that the physicists knew enough to stand in one place and just move their feet while the women danced around them. When one of the dancers made her way through the tables to perform in front of Stephen Hawking, however, I thought we might be crossing the boundary conditions into bad taste. Here was a young woman stomping her feet and ruffling her plumage in front of a man who could barely move. I shouldn't have worried. Hawking grinned and moved his chair back and forth in his own version of flamenco. Nonseriousness triumphed.

When Murray and I made our farewell to Juan the next morning, I told him I realized that the media had focused on Stephen Hawking to the exclusion of everything else. I wanted him to know that, in appreciation of the stupendous experience, my own piece would concentrate on the theme of the conference and the relevance of the Coto Doñana.

WHEN I RETURNED HOME, everything from quantum decoherence to Dartford warblers still resonating, I was faced with the bill: I would have to write this up as a feature for *American Way*. I reread the contract for guidance. My length limit was 3,500 words and the manuscript was to be called "String Theory." I didn't worry about the latter, for contract titles never got used.

Because the story had landed me in territory not normally serviced by in-flights, I thought about *American Way* itself. On the one hand, its editors despised the other in-flights, commissioned features from Calvin Trillin and Carlos Fuentes, and had won magazine awards in categories dominated by *Esquire* and *Vanity Fair*. On the other hand, those same editors referred to their product as "the magazine next to the barf bag." I decided that the only solution was to give them more than they asked for. If I was faithful to the material and the material was persuasive, perhaps they would allow me the space of two features instead of one. I had, after all, an obligation to the photographer's photos as well; if the piece was killed, the shots wouldn't see print. What I came up with was far less than what I really wanted to write. I realized that the physics would come off as gibberish to the frequent flyer, since much of it sounded like gibberish to me as well; I toned the science way down and radically simplified, leaving a few outrageous statements for color. Unlike every other journalist in attendance, I would not focus exclusively on Stephen Hawking. He would be present, but only as part of the larger picture, a stance I shared with Juan. I cut and condensed the rest of the material, waxing professional, wincing at the shorn detail, and mailed it in hoping for the best.

A few days later I got a call from the features editor at Big Beige, as he called company headquarters at the Dallas–Fort Worth airport. "I'll lay it on the line. We consider ourselves smarter than our readers and we don't understand this piece."

I was disappointed but not unprepared for this. "Perhaps you could suggest some way to rework it."

"At that length? On such an esoteric subject? There's no point. But we do have another solution." I waited, listening. "We'd like you to cut it back to a department piece on Hawking. No other subject matter. Just Hawking."

Now I was really silent. Jeffrey wouldn't get his pictures printed. The conference and Coto Doñana wouldn't get their stories told. Worst of all, it would humiliate me to Juan, since I had said that this was just what I would avoid. On the other hand, I had signed a contract and *American Way* had paid for the trip. I felt I had no choice. I agreed to it. What ran was a 1,500-word piece consisting of the flour-child scene, purged of detail that might upset passengers who were dining, followed by the flamenco scene. Called "Dancing with Time," it proved my most popular piece for *American Way*. A speech therapy organization reprinted it in their journal and the State of California requested permission to use it on their College Board exam. Only the author felt chagrined.

But surely that wasn't the end. I had my notes and the half measure *American Way* didn't use. Someday I would go back to it, let it expand to its natural length and try to get it right. I would write for that frequent flyer, the common reader. I would try to gather the arrows.

I would return to the thermodynamic arrow. This was the one about entropy, that said that the universe was increasingly disordered as it aged. One of its passing orders was a cork forest with a complex, locally evolved ecosystem. That order began to unravel when the cork oaks were cut down and replaced with eucalyptus trees. There was an ongoing attempt to reverse the arrow, to bring the cork oak ecosystem back by growing new oaks under new pines, but it wouldn't re-create the lost ecosystem any more than the shattered wineglass would reassemble itself and leap back onto the table. A parallel instance of the thermodynamic arrow was the Coto Doñana, where a marsh had been turned into rice paddies, where water was being infused with pesticides and siphoned off to grow strawberries, and where the most important stop in Europe for migrating birds was being fractured and shrunk. Juan had voted against the existence of time, but he had directed the conference toward the Coto Doñana as a conservationist act, to aim Doñana toward a better future. Juan was trying to stave off the increase of entropy, to deflect the thermodynamic arrow.

I would make brief mention of the eschatological arrow, an unprogrammed arrow evoked by this journey. This locally popular asymmetry, which pointed to the Last Judgment, decreed that anyone who had not been baptized was doomed for eternity. The physicists had not collected that arrow, and I didn't either. There was evidence enough before us of the increase of entropy without judgment in the form of a wasting disease. The sufferer of that disease had concluded that black holes don't, in fact, swallow forever everything that reaches them, but gradually use up the mass of the black hole, sending particles back into the universe—and to the extent that Hawking was a hapless incarnation of his theory, he, too, threw off continuing ideas and sparks of life as he physically withdrew. His was an inspiring example of our common fight to hold our own as disorder increases.

I would quote the statement of a physicist named Iwo Białynicki-Birula. "Music has time duration. There is no instantaneous state of music. That is my instance of the glories of time asymmetry." I would leave the frequent flyer with the image of other creatures that flew, the black vultures that held their place in the wind through hundreds of small adjustments of their wings and tails. As complex adaptive systems, vultures could occur only as the universe expanded, and thus agreed with the cosmological arrow; and the organizational process that created them threw off heat and increased overall disorder, agreeing with the thermodynamic arrow. But I wasn't so sure that they agreed with my psychological arrow, the third time asymmetry recognized by the physicists at the conference, the one that gives us a sense that the past gives way to the future as we go through our day. Neither advancing nor retreating, yet never motionless, those ancient and glorious birds seemed to stay in place even as the universe declined around them.

A NOTE ABOUT THE AUTHOR

Bruce Berger grew up in suburban Chicago. A poet and a nonfiction writer, he is best known for a series of books exploring the intersections of nature and culture in desert settings. The first of these, *The Telling Distance*, won the 1990 Western States Book Award and the 1992 Colorado Book Award. His articles and essays have appeared in *The New York Times*, *Sierra*, *Orion Magazine*, *Gramophone*, and numerous literary quarterlies; his poems have appeared in *Poetry*, *Barron's*, and various literary reviews in the United States, Scotland, and India, and have been collected in *Facing the Music*.